# Unfaithful
## Desires

Book Two

# Unfaithful
## Desires

Book Two
## Luke Andrew

A Little Passionate Tale Woven from Gossip—Some Whisper It's True

## Copyright

**The Unfaithful Desires – Book Two**

Luke Andrew

First Edition, 2025

© Luke Andrew, 2025. All rights reserved.

No part of this publication may be reproduced, stored in a retrieval system, or transmitted in any form or by any means—electronic, mechanical, photocopying, recording, or otherwise—without the author's or publisher's prior written permission.

This is a work of fiction. Names, characters, places, incidents, and dialogues are products of the author's imagination or used fictitiously. Any resemblance to actual persons, living or deceased, events, or locations is entirely coincidental. The narrative, dialogue, and incidents are products of the author's imagination and crafted solely for entertainment. No harm, offence, or misrepresentation is intended toward any individual, group, culture, or entity.

**Content Warning:**

This book contains mature themes, explicit content, and intimate depictions of adult relationships. It is intended for readers of legal age in their respective jurisdictions. Reader discretion is strongly advised.

The story explores complex and sensitive topics designed to provoke thought and reflection, not to replicate or comment on real-world experiences or events.

Readers should note that any similarities between fictional elements in this work and real-world references are unintended and should not be interpreted as factual or indicative of actual events, individuals, or places.

This work does not provide professional advice or commentary on any subject.

Requests for permission or inquiries should be directed to the author.

**ISBN : 978-93-343-2279-8**

# Contents

## The Past: Entwined In Time - Part II

| | | |
|---|---|---|
| #1 | A Lingering Spark | 1 |
| #2 | Boy To A Man | 21 |
| #3 | Fated In The Stars | 47 |
| #4 | Boundaries and Curves | 53 |
| #5 | Restless for You | 67 |
| #6 | Where There's Will, There's a Way | 75 |
| #7 | The Silent Connection | 91 |
| #8 | When Desire Rules | 97 |
| #9 | Between Family and Secrets | 111 |
| #10 | The Weight of Secrets and Goodbyes | 121 |

## The Present: Desire Untamed - Part II

| | | |
|---|---|---|
| #11 | Chossing Happiness | 137 |
| #12 | Beneath the Surface | 145 |
| #13 | Surrender to Desire | 153 |
| #14 | Heart's Call | 167 |
| #15 | The Calm Before the Storm | 173 |
| #16 | The Lies We Live | 183 |

## Gossip – Some say it was true

**Available On Most Online Stores**

## FICTIONAL

Milo the Cat – A Day Out

Villy the Vulture

Jeron and John – High and Fly

Ben the Bear

Who's in the ATTIC

Adventures of Binny n Bonny

Bella's Boat Escapade

Tales of the Mochi Wala – The Cobbler

Silence Whispers

## NON-FICTIONAL

Decoding Maturity

Navigating The Grey

I Lack Patience

# Prologue

**A Woman Unbound**

She was a woman of fire and longing—bound by duty yet haunted by desire. She was a wife, a mother, a woman yearning for more. Her love was deep, her devotion unquestionable, but the ache within her was undeniable.

For years, she had played the role expected of her. She had been the perfect wife, the devoted mother, the quiet shadow behind a husband who saw only what he wanted to see. But beneath the surface, cracks had begun to form. And when the truth of his infidelities reached her, the last thread of restraint snapped.

Betrayal did not break her—it awakened her.

She did not seek revenge, nor did she desire destruction. What she craved was something far more primal, more intoxicating—a connection that would ignite her soul. She found it in fleeting glances, whispered promises, and hands that trembled against her skin. The thrill of secrecy, the rush of forbidden desire—it was a hunger she could no longer ignore.

But passion is never without consequence.

What began as an escape soon became an obsession. The fire she had rekindled within herself threatened to consume everything—her marriage, reputation, and sense of self. She had entered a world where love and lust blurred and loyalty and longing warred against each other. And once she had tasted that freedom, how could she ever return?

Yet the past is never indeed left behind.

As whispers of scandal grew louder and shadows of guilt crept closer, she was forced to confront a question she had long ignored—was she genuinely seeking love or merely running from loneliness? And when the man she had once given everything to finally turned his gaze back to her, she had to wonder—could broken trust ever be rebuilt, or had she already strayed too far?

This is a tale of a marriage unravelled by secrets and deception, where love and betrayal walk hand in hand. It follows a woman torn between duty and desire, caught in a battle between what she should do and what she craves.

At its core, this love story is laced with temptation, obsession, and the undeniable pull of the forbidden. But every indulgence comes at a cost; the deeper she falls, the higher the price.

*Sensual. Thrilling. Unapologetic. Are you ready to step into the fire?*

## Unfaithful Desires Book One – A Recap

Yolaine had spent years trapped in a marriage that appeared enviable from the outside but was hollow within. She had been a loyal wife, a devoted mother, and a woman who had given everything to a relationship that never truly nourished her. Her marriage to Pierce had been built on fragile foundations—partly arranged by her parents, partly a mistake of youth. Back then, she had been captivated by his charm, promises of security, and the illusion of a man deeply in love with her.

Pierce had, in many ways, fulfilled his promises—he provided wealth, comfort, and stability. But beneath the polished veneer of a perfect husband, he was a man who led two lives. In one, he played the devoted family man; in the other, he indulged in his desires, betraying the vows he had sworn to uphold. Yolaine had spent years convincing herself that his occasional distance and unexplained absences were part of their life together. But deep down, she had always known.

His final betrayal shattered the illusion entirely. This time, there were no more excuses, no more second chances. The husband she had sacrificed so much for had never indeed been hers.

Lost and aching for something real, Yolaine was drawn to a man she could never have—Aston, a young seminarian bound by faith and duty. Their connection was unexpected, a stolen moment of quiet understanding in the dimly lit corridors of the church she often visited with her daughter. At first, it was innocent—exchanged glances, hushed conversations, an unspoken longing that neither dared to name. But desire is rarely silent for long.

Restraint crumbled in the sanctuary of shadows, where vows were meant to be sacred. It was not love that pulled them together but a desperate need—an unquenched hunger that neither of them had the strength to resist. His hands trembled against her skin, torn between devotion and desire, but in the heat of forbidden passion, all else faded. For the first time in years, Yolaine felt seen, felt wanted. Morality, faith, and consequences all dissolved in the fire of their reckless union.

But secrets never remain hidden forever.

Janice, Yolaine's closest friend, uncovered the affair and confronted her, torn between frustration and concern. She reminded Yolaine of the past—the reckless choices, the mistakes, the messes she had cleaned up before. And now, history was repeating itself. "Think of Kaley. Think of what will happen if Pierce finds out."

But Yolaine refused to be shamed. She had endured too much and sacrificed too much. "And what about me?" she countered. "What about everything I have suffered through? Everything I have lost?"

The mention of loss reopened old wounds. Before Aston, before Pierce's repeated betrayals and the game he played, Eugene had been there—Pierce's younger brother. Pierce had conveniently managed to break them up, though little did she know at the time.

Eugene had been the man she truly loved—who had supported her when she needed it most. When her world was falling apart, he had been her anchor, the one who saw her pain and carried it as his own. But in the end, she had chosen duty over love. She had convinced herself that Pierce had changed, that there was still something worth saving in their marriage. So, she walked away from Eugene, turning her back on the only man who had ever truly put her first.

Eugene didn't beg. He didn't fight. He walked away, knowing he couldn't hold on to a woman who hadn't chosen him completely. Later, she discovered that Pierce had deliberately orchestrated their separation by using Kaley as leverage. Pierce didn't want Yolaine to return to Eugene for good. He had to win, no matter the cost. He knew that Yolaine had been close to Eugene again, and they were growing closer. So, he returned from Denmark, leaving his affairs behind, to ensure that Yolaine and Eugene didn't get back together. When Yolaine discovered the truth, she was crushed. But Eugene was no longer there—he had left for good. Janice had always believed that Yolaine had made the right decision. "It was for the best," she had said back then, and she repeated it now. "You can't have two brothers fighting over you."

Yolaine responded, "Well, thanks to Pierce, he knew I liked his brother Eugene. But he manipulated Kaley so well that I had no choice but to give in for Kaley's sake." She exhaled sharply, her voice laced with the bitterness of old wounds. "Pierce doesn't love us. He doesn't like to lose. He will do anything to win. I know how he thinks."

Janice kept quiet. Yolaine knew the truth—Pierce had never been worth the sacrifice. When the truth about Pierce's latest infidelity surfaced—this time, through the voice of another woman who had finally decided to step forward—Yolaine knew she was done. She packed her bags, took Kaley, and left behind the ruins of a marriage that had never been a partnership.

Seeking refuge in the familiarity of her childhood home, she found an unexpected presence—Glen, her younger cousin and lifelong confidant. He, too, had come seeking solace, his heart weighed down by unspoken grief. The boy she once knew had grown into a man who understood her pain and saw her in a way no one else ever had.

At first, their bond was a source of comfort—two wounded souls leaning on each other in an unkind world. But the boundaries of family and friendship blurred in the quiet moments between them. Grief and desire became intertwined, and what began as innocent solace soon ignited something far more dangerous.

One night, restraint was abandoned in the depths of longing and loneliness. Glen's touch was unlike any she had known—tender yet urgent, reverent yet desperate. And in his arms, Yolaine surrendered.

But passion, like fate, is never without consequence.

## What to Expect in Book Two of Unfaithful Desires

A deeper, more intricate web of love, betrayal, and forbidden passion begins to unravel. When Janice discovers that Yolaine is now involved with another man—Aston—she confronts her friend, drawing painful parallels to Yolaine's former entanglement with Glen. That affair nearly destroyed Yolaine's marriage once before, and Janice fears history may be repeating itself. As accusations fly and old wounds are reopened, blame is laid bare. Janice pleads with Yolaine not to lose herself in yet another dangerous affair.

But Yolaine refuses to be swayed—neither by Janice's warnings nor society's judgment. She has lived a life marked by loyalty, commitment, and quiet sacrifice, only to be repaid with heartbreak, betrayal, and a crushing sense of worthlessness. No longer. This time, she chooses desire over duty. She clarifies to Janice that she will not walk away if Aston wants to be with her. She will no longer abandon her happiness to meet the expectations of others.

Yolaine confesses that what happened with Glen was a moment of weakness—a desperate need for comfort when Pierce, her husband, betrayed her trust. Though Pierce made amends and tried to be a better husband and father, it wasn't long before he slipped back into his old ways. And it was then that Yolaine realised she deserved more. A life where she is cared for, valued, and given the time and attention she had been denied for far too long.

She knows how to balance her life with her daughter. And if Pierce could destroy their marriage, take her for granted, and betray her unwavering loyalty after years of devotion, then choosing to live life on her terms is a decision she no longer feels guilty for making.

Janice still wants the best for Yolaine—even if they no longer see eye to eye.

As we delve deeper into the past in Entwined In Time – Part II, the whole story of Yolaine and Glen is laid bare—their forbidden affair, shared desires, and the regrets that haunt them both. Meanwhile, in the present, Desire Untamed – Part II explores Yolaine's consuming connection with Aston—the man torn between his priesthood and his undeniable craving for her. A man who may offer her the love she's always longed for… or break her in a way no one else ever has.

And where does Pierce fit into it all? Will he uncover the truth about her affair? And if he does, what will he do? Will he fight to regain Yolaine and repair the life he so carelessly shattered? Or will his sins and selfishness consume him before he ever has the chance?

In Unfaithful Desires: Book Two, the tension builds, and the stakes have never been higher. Love, lust, and loyalty collide in a battle none can outrun. One decision. One moment. And everything will change.

The truth is coming—and when it does, it will leave nothing but destruction.

Yolaine looked forward to living boldly and provocatively, embracing life on her terms. She sought places where she was wanted, loved, and free to be herself.

# The Past
# Entwined In Time
## Part II

## #1
# A Lingering Spark

The afternoon sun cast golden hues through the sheer curtains, draping the house in a warm, dreamlike glow. Yolaine barely noticed. Her thoughts were elsewhere—on the soft laughter echoing outside, the hum of a motorcycle engine that had long since quieted, and the presence of a man who stirred something deep and dangerous within her.

Glen had taken Kaley out for a ride, and when they returned, her daughter's pockets bulged with sweets and chocolates, her innocent delight oblivious to the silent exchange that passed between the adults in the room. Yolaine, busy in the kitchen, caught glimpses of them through the doorway, her hands working on muscle memory as her mind wandered to something far less innocent.

As Glen stepped inside, Yolaine's voice was calm but firm. "Kaley, go to your grandmother and wash up." Her daughter obeyed without protest, skipping toward the kitchen with a giggle. Yolaine wiped her hands on a cloth, steadying herself before returning to the living room.

Glen was still there, standing near the doorway as if he was caught between staying and leaving. His gaze flickered over her before he smirked, shifting on his feet.

"What?" he asked, his tone teasing.

Yolaine arched an eyebrow but said nothing.

Glen tilted his head. "What?" he repeated, amusement lacing his voice. "Why are you staring at me?"

She crossed her arms, tilting her chin up slightly. "Kaley isn't supposed to have so many sweets and chocolates," she said softly. "Don't spoil her."

Glen let out an exaggerated sigh. "Ohhh… got it. I'll remember that next time." He stretched lazily, feigning nonchalance. "I should go for a stroll," he added, moving toward the door, avoiding her gaze.

Yolaine reached out, catching his wrist before he could step out. Her touch was light, but the effect was electric. He froze.

"Where are you going?" she asked, voice barely above a whisper.

Glen hesitated, then shrugged. "Just a walk."

"Alone?" she probed, eyes glinting with mischief.

He chuckled, finally looking at her. "Who else would join me? I don't know anyone here."

Yolaine smirked. "Last night, you seemed to be getting acquainted just fine."

He caught the insinuation instantly, his grin widening. "Oh, so you were paying attention?"

Before she could answer, the abrupt knock at the door shattered the moment. Yolaine's heart stilled as she turned toward the entrance. A visitor. Unexpected. Janice.

Glen stepped back slightly, his playful smirk replaced with a guarded expression. Yolaine exhaled, smoothing her dress as she moved toward the door, a sense of unease creeping over her.

Destiny was playing games and wasn't sure if she was winning or losing.

"Janice... what a surprise. What brings you here?" Yolaine's voice dripped with sarcasm, her expression a mix of displeasure and unease. Of all people, Janice was the last person she wanted to see right now.

"I was visiting my mum and dad, and I heard you were here too," Janice said, her eyes flicking around with keen interest. "When did you arrive? Is Pierce with you? And—who's this?"

The questions poured out, one after another. It was precisely why Yolaine went out of her way to avoid Janice. Her nosiness was relentless, her love for gossip insatiable. Beneath it all, Yolaine knew there was jealousy—Janice had always resented the way men, young and old, seemed drawn to her.

"I came a few days ago," Yolaine replied coolly. "I'm here with Kaley to visit Mum and Dad, but they're away. Only Grandma's home."

Janice barely acknowledged the response—her attention was elsewhere. She kept glancing at the young man standing in the doorway, his striking features impossible to ignore. The curiosity burned in her eyes.

"And who's this handsome bloke?" she finally asked, unable to contain herself.

Glen exchanged a knowing look with Yolaine and smirked, choosing to remain silent. He had been watching their exchange with quiet amusement.

"That's Glen, my cousin. He's visiting." Yolaine's tone was deliberately dismissive, offering nothing more.

Janice expected a further explanation, but none came. That only made her more suspicious.

Still hovering in the doorway, she eventually stepped inside, heading straight for the kitchen, where she found Yolaine's grandmother. With a warm greeting, Janice quickly slipped into conversation, her real intent clear—she wanted information.

"So, what's Glen doing here?" she asked casually, fishing for details.

The older woman smiled. *"Oh, he's just visiting. The poor boy had his heart broken, so he came to spend some time with us. Yolaine arrived around the same time—it's nice to have people around the house again. I do miss the company."*

Janice nodded, storing away the details, but something still didn't sit right with her.

Much later, as Janice finally left, Yolaine exhaled in relief. She always found her exhausting—too prying, too calculating. She knew this wouldn't be the last of Janice's digging. But for now, she was glad to be rid of her.

As evening settled, Yolaine was alone with Glen in the living room. She had meant to talk to him about their awkwardness, the unspoken tension lingering for days. But her words faltered as she glanced at him—his tousled hair, his relaxed posture.

He stepped closer, reaching for the remote, and in doing so, his fingers lightly brushed against her arm. A spark flickered between them. It was a slight, fleeting touch, yet it shivered through her. Neither of them moved, and neither of them spoke.

It felt like the world had stilled briefly, holding its breath with her.

And then—

"Glen! Come play with me!"

Kaley burst into the room, climbing onto the couch between them with all the energy of a child blissfully unaware that she had just interrupted something.

Glen chuckled, letting the tension slip away as he turned to her. "Alright, let's go," he said, exaggeratingly lifting her.

Kaley squealed with delight as he carried her outside into the garden.

Yolaine watched them from the doorway, a soft smile tugging at her lips. Something about seeing Glen like this—lighthearted and carefree—made her heart flutter. Shaking off the thought, she turned away and headed to the kitchen to help her grandmother.

## A Lingering Spark

That night, after Kaley had dozed off in Yolaine's bed, sleep refused to come to her. The house was quiet except for the distant hum of the television.

Slipping out of bed, she checked in on her grandmother, who was fast asleep, before quietly wandering into the living room.

Glen was stretched out on his makeshift bed, the dim glow of the TV flickering over his face. The soft rise and fall of his breathing made it seem like he might fall asleep at any moment.

She dropped onto the couch beside him. "What are you watching?"

"Cartoons," he replied, his gaze fixed on the screen.

She raised an eyebrow. "Cartoons? You do realise you're practically a cartoon character yourself?"

His head snapped toward her, feigning offence. "Excuse me?!"

She grinned. "Oh, you heard me."

Without warning, he grabbed a pillow and tossed it at her.

She gasped, catching it just in time. "Oh, now you've done it!" she declared, launching the pillow back at him.

What started as a playful toss quickly escalated into an all-out battle. Laughter filled the room as they wrestled, pillows flying in every direction. Glen, stronger than her, managed to pin her arms down as she struggled beneath him.

"Not so tough now, are you?" he teased, smirking.

Yolaine huffed, feigning defeat before suddenly wriggling free. She sat up, catching her breath as he fell back against the couch, still grinning.

Still playful, she moved behind him and ruffled his hair. "Messy as always," she teased.

Glen groaned, stretching lazily. "Since you're back there, you might as well give me a head massage."

She scoffed. "Yeah, because I signed up to be your masseuse."

Before she could pull away, Glen grabbed her wrist and tugged—too hard.

She lost her balance, tumbling forward until her forehead bumped against his.

"Ow!" Yolaine yelped, instantly bringing a hand to her lip. A sharp sting—she'd bitten it on impact.

Glen spun around, his eyes widening. "Oh, crap—are you okay?"

She winced, touching her lip. "My lip, you idiot!"

He bolted upright, rushing off before returning with water and a cotton pad. "Here, let me see."

Yolaine pouted dramatically. "First you injured me, now you wanna play nurse? What kind of treatment is this?"

He chuckled, kneeling beside her. "I feel terrible, okay? Let me make it up to you."

With that, he leaned in and placed a feather-light kiss on her cheek. Then another.

Yolaine froze, her breath catching. The teasing air between them shifted, the playfulness melting into something softer.

Then, slowly, he brushed his lips against hers.

She didn't pull away.

And in that quiet moment, she realised—maybe she didn't want to.

His touch was gentle, nothing like the hunger she had grown accustomed to with Pierce. With Pierce, love had always felt like an obligation, a routine, a means to an end. He touched her when he wanted, kissed her when it suited him and held her only to satisfy himself.

But Glen—

Glen was different. His touch wasn't claiming. It was asking. Seeking.

And for the first time in a long time, she felt something unfamiliar bloom in her chest.

The kind of warmth that didn't demand.

The kind of affection that… was.

The air between Yolaine and Glen crackled with unspoken tension as the evening deepened. The dim glow of the television flickered across the room, casting shifting shadows over their forms. Yolaine, perched on the couch, reached over and playfully ruffled Glen's hair, her fingers tangling briefly in the soft strands.

"You're such a duffer," she teased, her voice light but her eyes dark with something else.

Glen smirked, turning his gaze toward her. "That I am," he admitted, his grin boyish, disarming.

Yolaine leaned in closer, her lips just a whisper away from his ear. "Are you just going to talk, or are you going to do something?" Her breath, warm and teasing, sent a shiver down his spine.

Glen swallowed hard, his pulse hammering. He turned his face toward hers, their noses almost touching. "I want you," he whispered hoarsely, his voice raw with need. "Can I have you?"

A slow, knowing smile played on Yolaine's lips. "Do you think you're ready?" she murmured back, her tone full of wicked promise.

She took his hands, guiding them to the hem of her nightgown, encouraging and showing him what she wanted. Glen hesitated briefly before gathering the fabric and slowly lifting it upward. The material slid over her thighs and then her hips, revealing smooth, bare skin beneath. His breath hitched—she wasn't wearing anything underneath.

His fingers traced the curve of her waist, then slid lower, over the soft swell of her core. His touch was tentative as if committing every inch of her to memory. Yolaine leaned into him, pressing closer, her voice a whisper against his lips.

"Touch me," she urged, guiding his hands over her.

The nightgown slipped higher, exposing the swell of her breasts, her nipples tightening under the cool air. Glen swallowed hard, mesmerised. He reached up, cupping her in his hands, squeezing gently, and feeling her soft weight in his palms.

"You're so soft," he murmured, awed. His thumbs brushed over her nipples, rolling them experimentally. "And you smell so good."

Yolaine gasped, arching into his touch. "Do you like how I feel?" she whispered, teasing.

Yolaine helped him remove his t-shirt while he was still wearing his half-jeans. Though his shaft was visibly stiff by now, Glen barely noticed anything but her—her scent, her warmth, the way she surrendered to his touch.

He pressed his lips to her collarbone, then trailed downward, his breath warm against her skin. His mouth found one of her nipples, tongue flicking against the peak before drawing it between his lips. Yolaine moaned, fingers burying in his hair, urging him closer.

He lavished attention on her, switching between each nipple, his hands kneading, squeezing, exploring as if he'd never touched a woman before—because he hadn't, not like this, not with this level of aching reverence.

"I love how you taste," he whispered against her skin, his voice husky, raw.

Yolaine hummed in pleasure, threading her fingers through his hair. "Then don't stop," she breathed, guiding him lower. Glen needed this encouragement. He explored her more, though he had had her last night. This was his second time with her, yet it felt like the first—like he was discovering something sacred, something forbidden and intoxicating.

Glen's hands travelled downward, fingers tracing the curve of her hips, then slipping between her thighs, exploring with the same hungry curiosity. Then, moving to her small but firm backside, her bottoms, she arched more so he could caress further. He held it in his hands and squeezed them, a slight, naughty spank following. She giggled. "You're getting bolder," she said.

He grinned, his confidence swelling.

8

The passion between them ignited, slow and smouldering, building toward something inevitable, something unstoppable. In the hush of the night, with nothing but the flickering glow of the television and their mingling breaths, they surrendered to the undeniable pull between them.

Glen effortlessly picked up Yolaine, carrying her to the makeshift bed in the living room. He laid her on her back, his gaze roaming over her as she lifted her hands, inviting him closer. A playful smirk curved her lips, a silent beckoning.

He stepped back briefly, slipping out of his half-jean trousers, and his shaft sprang free. Yolaine's eyes darkened with desire as she whispered, "Someone is steamy…" in a low, sultry voice.

"I never knew it could grow this long," Glen murmured with a grin, slowly crawling over her, their bodies inching closer until there was no space between them.

She spread her legs wide, welcoming him, her body an open invitation. His eyes traced the smooth curves of her fold, the way her thighs framed the glistening slit between them. As he moved closer, she reached for his shaft, guiding him toward her folds. He had never seen such smooth, clean-shaven skin before—perhaps in movies or magazines, but never in reality. This was something else entirely. It was only the second time he had seen her like this, yet it still felt fresh and new, as if he were discovering her again.

His fingers trailed down, grazing over her folds, feeling the soft heat beneath them. She shivered, parting her thighs even more expansive, granting him full access and inviting him to explore her without hesitation.

The heat between them was intoxicating. As he pressed into her, her soft walls enveloped him, slick and inviting, allowing him to sink deep within her in one fluid thrust. A gasp escaped her lips as she wrapped her legs tightly around his waist, pulling him closer and locking them together.

Their mouths met in a searing kiss; moans muffled between them. Glen set a slow, steady rhythm; each thrust sending waves of pleasure through her body. Yolaine shut her eyes, lost in the sensation and carried away by the raw passion surging between them.

The flickering light from the television cast soft shadows across their entwined bodies, the cartoon noises in the background masking the sounds of their shared pleasure. Glen scurried, his strokes deep and unrelenting, making Yolaine tremble beneath him.

"You feel incredible," she whispered breathlessly.

Glen chuckled against her lips. "I guess I'm a natural."

She grinned, her fingers digging into his back as he drove into her again, the pleasure building with each movement. Seconds melted into minutes, his stamina unwavering as he took her over and over again.

Her body responded eagerly, her folds tightening around him, urging him deeper. She had never felt this way; his youthful energy and unyielding rhythm were overwhelming and addictive.

"Are you okay?" Glen murmured, brushing a damp strand of hair from her face.

"Yes... yes... don't stop," she whispered, her voice laced with desperation.

He obeyed, thrusting into her once more, his movements controlled yet primal. Yolaine clung to him, her body surrendering entirely to the pleasure, to the way he made love to her—slow, deep, and relentless.

Their lips met in a fervent kiss, tongues tangling, moans swallowed between them. Glen set a slow rhythm, each movement deliberate, each thrust more profound than the last. Yolaine arched against him, her fingers tracing over his back, nails lightly grazing his skin, urging him on.

"Glen..." she breathed against his lips, her voice a plea. "Take me... take all of me."

A shiver ran through him at her words, his need for her growing insatiable. His rhythm deepened, his movements unrelenting. The muted glow of the television flickered across their entwined bodies, its distant chatter masking the sinful melody of their pleasure.

Yolaine's hands drifted to her breasts, teasing the sensitive peaks as she moaned beneath him. She tilted her head, guiding his lips downward, whispering against his ear, "Take one in your mouth... I want to feel you there."

A deep growl rumbled in Glen's chest as he obeyed, his lips descending to capture one of her hardened peaks. He suckled her hungrily, his tongue tracing languid circles, drawing sharp gasps from her lips. The dual sensation of his mouth worshipping her, his body claiming her, sent her spiralling into a haze of ecstasy.

She clung to him, her fingers tangled in his hair, pressing him closer, needing more. Glen's hands gripped her waist as he drove into her with renewed intensity, his breath hot against her skin, their bodies moving in perfect sync.

"You taste so good," he murmured, his voice thick with desire as he lifted his head to kiss her again. Their lips crashed together, the passion between them searing, desperate.

Seconds blurred into minutes, the world outside them ceasing to exist. She had never felt this way—utterly consumed, completely alive in his arms.

She could feel Glen reaching his limit, his body trembling against hers as he fought to hold back. His thrusts grew erratic and desperate, and his breath ragged against her skin. Every stroke drove her deeper into pleasure, their bodies slick with heat and desire, their connection undeniable.

"Don't hold it," she murmured, her fingers caressing his damp back, feeling the strain in his muscles as he tried to prolong the inevitable. "Let it go... release it into me."

His lips hovered near her ear, his voice strained with pleasure. "Are you sure?"

She nodded, tightening her legs around his waist, pulling him even more profoundly, her warmth wrapped around him, urging him to give in completely. "Yes… take me, claim me, love. We have the whole night ahead of us. As much as you want, again and again."

At her words, Glen groaned deeply, his entire body tensing as the last of his restraints shattered. With one final thrust, he buried himself to the hilt, his release spilling into her in hot waves. His head fell against her shoulder, his breath coming in heavy, uneven gasps as he emptied himself inside her, filling her.

Yolaine gasped at the sensation, her body trembling as she felt his warmth spread deep within her. Even though they had surrendered to their passion just the night before, the sheer intensity of his release startled her—the heat of him, the way he poured himself into her with such urgency and hunger. She had never felt so claimed, so consumed.

Glen remained inside her, his body still pulsing with the aftershocks of pleasure, his arms wrapped around her as if he never wanted to let go. His lips brushed over her collarbone and neck before he whispered against her skin, "You feel incredible…" His voice was thick, heavy with satisfaction.

Yolaine smiled breathlessly, tracing her fingers through his damp hair and pressing a lingering kiss to his temple. "And we've only just begun…"

Yolaine knew precisely what she was getting into but didn't want to consider it. Right now, she just wanted to indulge in Glen, to savour every moment. The woman in her longed to feel wanted, loved, cherished, and caressed. She craved the touch she had been starving for.

She had made many mistakes in her life—wrong choices and painful sacrifices. She lost Eugene twice, each time giving up her happiness for her family. She thought Pierce would feel remorse for his actions, but nothing changed. Now, none of that mattered.

She just wanted to feel alive.

This was never planned. Glen and Yolaine were cousins, and they never thought they would become entangled in such an emotional bond. And yet, they were—leaning on each other, offering the support neither had found elsewhere.

It may be wrong. Maybe they shouldn't be involved physically. But who else could understand them better than someone they had known since childhood? Someone they were comfortable with. Someone who would keep their secret safe.

Let passion drive them now.

What comes next... they would figure out later.

They lay next to each other, their bodies still warm from the intensity of their passion. Yolaine rested her head on Glen's chest, both grinning like mischievous teenagers. His hand lazily traced over her curves, caressing the smooth expanse of her waist and her hip, his fingers teasing the sensitive spots that made her shiver.

She tilted slightly, giving him more access, her body melting into his touch as they tangled together.

Glen smirked, letting his thoughts spill out. "Me and my cousin, stark naked next to each other... never in my wildest dreams did I think this day would come."

Yolaine's eyes snapped to his, amusement and mischief flickering within them. She grinned before giving him a playful smack on the head. "You're an absolute menace," she muttered. "I never dreamt of it either!"

He chuckled, rubbing the spot where she had hit him, then, with a wicked gleam in his eyes, slid his hands lower, teasing her skin with featherlight touches. His fingers danced along her sides, dipping into the hollows of her waist before trailing up to her ribs.

Yolaine gasped, her body jerking instinctively. "Glen, don't you dare—"

Too late. He attacked, tickling her mercilessly. She shrieked, wriggling beneath him, her laughter bubbling uncontrollably as she struggled to push his hands away.

"Shhh! You'll wake the whole house!" she whispered urgently between gasps, biting her lip to suppress another giggle.

"Well, Granny wouldn't even notice if there was an earthquake," Glen teased, still grinning. "The only one we need to worry about is Kaley—"

Before he could finish, a small voice pierced the air.

"Mama... Mama!"

Yolaine froze. Her heart jumped into her throat as she bolted upright, scrambling for her nightgown. Glen barely had time to smother his laughter before she threw it over herself and dashed to the bedroom.

Kaley sat up in bed, rubbing her sleepy eyes. Yolaine rushed to her side, smoothing her hair and whispering soothing words.

"Shhh, love. Go back to sleep; I'm here." She gently stroked her daughter's back, patting her rhythmically until her breathing ceased.

Meanwhile, Glen took the opportunity to slip into the bathroom, returning moments later. He dropped onto the couch, running a hand through his hair, still grinning.

It wasn't long before Yolaine reappeared, leaning against the doorframe with a smirk. The dim light bathed her in a golden hue, the loose fabric of her nightgown draping lazily over her curves. Glen lay on the couch, his bare chest exposed, half-jeans hanging low on his hips, watching her with a knowing smirk.

"So, where were we?" she asked playfully, stepping closer, her fingers grazing the armrest.

Glen stretched leisurely, his arms behind his head, his grin widening. "Well... we were both naked, and I was admiring my lovely cousin," he teased, voice rich with mischief.

She rolled her eyes but couldn't hide the amused curve of her lips. Their bond had always been strong—growing up together, sharing secrets, playing in Grandma's garden. That familiarity made it easy to sink into this newfound closeness, though the initial awkwardness of seeing each other fully exposed had sent a thrilling shiver through them. The boundary had been crossed, and there was no turning back.

"You're cheeky, Glen," she quipped, moving onto the couch and straddling his lap. Her hands caught his wrists, pinning them above his head, pressing him back into the cushions. "You said you liked to admire, love?" she whispered, her lips hovering just above his, her warm breath teasing his skin. "Then just sit back and admire."

He tensed beneath her as she rolled her hips just enough to make him inhale sharply. His fingers twitched, aching to touch, but she wouldn't let him.

"Yolaine…" His voice was strained, a warning laced with desire.

"Shh…" She pressed a single finger against his lips. "No talking. Just feel."

She pulled away suddenly, standing before him. With deliberate slowness, she let her nightgown slip from her shoulders, gliding down her soft skin before pooling at her feet. Glen's gaze darkened, his lips parting as he drank her in. The way his eyes followed every inch of her bare form sent a delicious thrill through her.

"You like to admire, don't you?" she teased, swaying slightly, fingers brushing over her curves.

Glen exhaled sharply. "You're playing a dangerous game, love."

She giggled, stepping closer, running the silky fabric of her nightgown over his face before tossing it aside. "Then let's see how long you can last."

Turning around, she faced the TV, her bare back exposed to him, the curves of her hips swaying subtly. When she turned back, she lifted one leg onto the couch, positioning herself just close enough that he could see her most intimate folds—so near, yet untouchable. His breath hitched, his restraint wavering.

Before she could react, Glen had already made up his mind. His eyes darkened with hunger, his breath uneven as he took her in—every curve, every inch of her bare skin beckoning him closer. He stripped away the last barrier between them, his arousal blatant, throbbing with need.

He reached for her, hands firm yet reverent, dragging her gently onto the bed before pinning her down beneath him. His weight pressed deliciously against her, his warmth sinking into her skin. Yolaine smirked, breathless, teasing, "I know you're strong, cousin."

A slow, wicked grin stretched across his lips. "You've yet to see just how strong."

His fingers skimmed her inner thighs, featherlight, teasing, drawing a shudder from her as he parted her legs. He took his time, relishing how she squirmed, desperate for him to claim her. When he finally guided himself to her entrance, his tip nudging against her slick folds, she tensed momentarily at a stretch, gasping.

"Easy, darling," she whispered, nails pressing into his shoulders. He paused just enough to brush his lips over hers before sinking in, inch by inch until he was fully seated within her. A groan rumbled deep in his chest as he disappeared inside her, engulfed in her heat.

He moved with slow, deliberate thrusts, dragging himself out only to plunge back in, each movement measured, torturous. She arched beneath him, spreading wider, inviting him deeper, guiding his inexperienced yet eager body. He was learning—learning how to take her, how to claim her properly.

Their bodies found a rhythm, a sinful dance of pleasure and longing. Kisses deepened, hands explored, their connection consuming them until nothing else existed beyond this moment. He couldn't get enough of her, of the way she felt, the way she gasped his name between moans.

She pressed her lips to his ear, breathless, her voice dripping with need. "Would you like to take me from behind?"

Glen groaned in response, his hands gripping her waist as she turned, arching her back, offering herself to him. She positioned a pillow beneath her stomach, elevating her hips, exposing the roundness of her bottom, her glistening core spread and waiting for him. She reached back, guiding him to her entrance once more.

He slid in slowly, the angle making her gasp, her fingers clutching the sheets. "Gentle," she whimpered, but Glen was already lost, overtaken by the sheer intensity of being inside her like this.

"I'll try," he muttered, voice thick with desire, "but I don't know if I can."

He began to move, slow at first, measured, but the sensation—the sight of her, the way she clenched around him—was overwhelming. He gripped her hips, thrusting deeper, unable to hold back, watching the way her body responded to him, how she took him so perfectly.

She moaned shamelessly, rocking back against him, matching his movements, craving every inch of him. He reached around, cupping her breast, teasing her stiffened nipple between his fingers while his other hand trailed lower, brushing against her most sensitive spot. She jerked at the added stimulation, crying out in pleasure.

He leaned forward, pressing his chest against her back, his breath hot against her ear. "You feel so good," he rasped, his thrusts turning erratic, desperate.

She was unravelling, trembling beneath him, pleasure coiling tight in her belly. "I can't... I can't hold back," she whimpered. "Take me. Fill me."

That was all he needed. His rhythm faltered as he buried himself deep, groaning her name as he reached his peak. His release flooded into her, her body welcoming every drop, her pleasure tipping her over the edge. She cried out, her entire body quaking as she clenched around him, pulling him deeper into her, keeping him there until every last pulse had shuddered through him.

Collapsing onto her, he buried his face against her shoulder, his breath ragged, his heart pounding against her back. They stayed like that, bodies tangled, lost in the aftermath of their passion.

Finally, Yolaine stirred, pressing a lazy kiss to his forehead. "Now, love," she murmured, "you should move."

With a reluctant groan, Glen rolled onto his side, watching as she shifted, removing the pillow and turning to face him. She cupped his face, tracing the sharp line of his jaw, studying him with something tender in her gaze. Then, with a soft, knowing smile, she kissed him—slow, lingering, filled with silent gratitude.

"Thank you," she whispered against his lips. "You've made me feel alive again."

Glen flushed at her words, his expression melting into something warm and vulnerable. He rested his head against her chest, listening to the steady rhythm of her heartbeat as they lay together in the quiet aftermath.

Yolaine was the first to rise, stretching, her body glowing from their encounter as she padded towards the bathroom. Glen lay back, watching her disappear behind the door, his body still thrumming with the reality of what had just happened.

And he knew—nothing would ever be the same again. His body was still thrumming with the aftershocks of what had just transpired, and his mind refused to quiet. His heart pounded—not from exertion but from the sheer weight of what had happened.

This wasn't just some reckless night of passion. It was Yolaine. The woman he had admired from a distance, the woman he had never thought he'd be close enough to touch, let alone claim in the way he just had.

He ran a hand through his damp hair, exhaling slowly. He had come here seeking solitude, a place to clear his head, to mend the fractures of a heartbroken elsewhere. But Yolaine had shattered every reason he had for staying away, for avoiding temptation. She had pulled him into something deeper, something he hadn't even realised he craved.

What did this mean for them? Would she regret it in the morning? Would she pull away, pretend it never happened?

A part of him wanted to believe this wasn't just an escape for her, that she felt the same fire he did. She wasn't just using him to forget the man who had betrayed her.

Because for him—this was different. This was everything.

Just then, Yolaine returned from the bathroom, her skin glowing in the dim light. She leaned down, pressing a soft kiss to Glen's forehead. It was tender, a quiet acknowledgement of what they had shared, yet it left him wanting more.

"Good night," she whispered.

Then, without another word, she slipped out of his room. Glen watched her go, listening to the faint rustle of sheets as she climbed into bed beside Kaley. Yolaine patted her daughter gently, comforted by the warmth of her little girl beside her. She exhaled a deep, contented sigh.

She was satisfied. She was at peace. She liked every bit of it.

Glen, on the other hand, lay awake, staring at the ceiling, his mind racing. His body ached to pull her back, to hold her through the night, to keep her close and safe in his arms. But instead, he forced himself to close his eyes, forcing back the emotions threatening to consume him.

Tonight, he had touched something untouchable. And he wasn't sure if he could ever let it go.

#2

# Boy To A Man

The early morning light filtered through the curtains, casting a golden glow over the tangled sheets. Glen stirred, his body heavy with the lingering warmth of the night before. He turned, instinctively reaching for Yolaine, but the space beside him was empty, the sheets cool.

The faint clatter of dishes and the unmistakable sound of Kaley chattering filled the air. The house was waking up. Glen lay there momentarily, staring at the ceiling, his mind hazy yet more apparent than ever. Something had changed. He was no longer the heartbroken young man who had come here to escape. He had tasted power, passion, and something deeper with Yolaine—something that had set a fire in his veins, something he craved more of.

He swung his legs off the bed and stood, stretching. He was still sore in places, a delicious ache reminding him of the night before. A slow smirk tugged at his lips as flashes of Yolaine's body, the way she melted beneath him, the way she moaned his name, played over in his mind. He exhaled sharply, raking a hand through his tousled hair before grabbing a pair of sweatpants and slipping them on.

The scent of coffee and breakfast hit him when he stepped out of the room. His stomach rumbled, but something else gnawed at him, something more substantial than hunger. He moved down the hall, drawn by an invisible pull.

Yolaine stood in the kitchen doorway, her arms folded, watching Kaley rummage through the fridge. She wore an oversized shirt, the hem skimming the tops of her thighs, her hair a tousled mess from sleep.

Glen's gaze roved over her. He could still see the faint marks on her skin—his marks—evidence of where his lips had been, where his hands had possessed her. She hadn't noticed him yet, and for a brief second, he let himself admire her, his body already stirring at the mere sight of her standing there, so effortlessly sensual.

As he moved past her, he deliberately brushed his shoulder against hers. The touch was fleeting but intentional. His bare skin met the soft fabric of her shirt, and he felt how she tensed, the slight intake of breath she tried to mask.

Yolaine didn't flinch. She didn't step back. Instead, she turned slightly, her lips curling in the faintest smirk.

She knew exactly what he had done. And she liked it.

Glen said nothing and walked into the kitchen, reaching for a glass of water as if last night hadn't stripped them to something raw and undeniable. But he could feel her watching him, the heat lingering between them.

He took a slow sip of water, letting the coolness settle the fire licking at his insides. This wasn't over. If anything, it had only just begun.

Every chance he got, he teased her. A fleeting touch to her waist as he walked by. A playful pinch to her hip when no one was looking. His lips barely grazed her ear as he murmured something utterly innocent yet wholly loaded with intent. Yolaine played along, but Glen could see it—the way her breath hitched, the way her body tensed ever so slightly, the way she wanted more.

And then, fate handed him a perfect opportunity.

Grandma took Kaley to the market after breakfast, leaving the house empty. The moment the door shut behind them, Glen didn't hesitate. He strode towards Yolaine with a wicked glint in his eyes, and before she could react, he scooped her into his arms.

"Glen!" she gasped, laughing as he carried her through the hallway.

He didn't stop until they reached her bedroom—a place he had never dared enter before. With a teasing smirk, he tossed her onto the bed before climbing in after her, his hands already reaching for her, his mouth claiming hers in a searing kiss.

She didn't resist. If anything, she kissed him back harder, her fingers sinking into his hair, her body arching into him.

"The living room doors are open," she murmured breathlessly between kisses. "Anyone could walk in."

That was enough to make Glen pause. He groaned, dropping his forehead to hers. "You're trying to kill me, woman."

She smirked, running her nails down his bare back. "Better hurry, then."

Glen bolted out of the room, locking the living room door from the inside. If Grandma and Kaley returned, they'd have to ring the bell. That bought him time—though not much. But he didn't need much.

The moment Glen rushed back into the bedroom, he froze. Yolaine lay sprawled across the sheets, her oversized shirt discarded, the lace of her panties pulled aside as if inviting him closer. The soft morning light kissed every curve of her bare skin, highlighting the slow rise and fall of her chest, the smoothness of her stomach, and the subtle dip between her thighs. She stretched lazily, fingers grazing her skin as if waiting for him.

A wicked, knowing smile curved on her lips. "Your time starts now."

His control snapped like a taut thread. With a low, hungry growl, Glen tore off his shirt and pulled down his shorts, his erection already painfully hard, aching for her. He was on her in seconds, pinning her beneath him, his mouth crashing onto hers in a kiss so profound it left them both gasping for air.

Yolaine moaned into the kiss, her nails digging into his back as she arched beneath him, pressing herself closer, needing more. His lips traced down her throat, over her collarbone, until they landed on one hardened nipple, his tongue swirling over it. She gasped, her back lifting off the mattress as he sucked harder. His free hand moved to the other breast, gently rolling it between his fingers, savouring the creamy softness beneath his touch.

"You're insatiable," she panted, her fingers tangled in his hair.

"And you love it," he murmured against her skin before trailing his tongue lower, his hands spreading her thighs.

Yolaine let out a breathy laugh, her body already responding, her folds slick and warm as she rocked against him. "Shut up and prove it."

Without hesitation, his fingers slid through the wetness between her thighs, teasing her before positioning himself at her entrance. In one deep thrust, he entered deeper into her, filling her completely, and both of them let out a strangled moan. She clenched around him, her body greedy, as if she'd been aching for this just as much as he had.

Glen groaned, gripping her hips, pushing her legs higher, folding her beneath him to go deeper. The new angle sent a jolt of pleasure through her, making her cry out. "That's it," he murmured against her lips, his rhythm relentless, each stroke making her tremble.

Her fingers dug into his shoulders, her breath coming in broken gasps as he drove her higher and higher. "You're getting—ah—so much better at this," she managed between moans, her body writhing beneath him.

Glen wasn't thinking anymore. He was lost in the taste of her, the feel of her, the way she tightened around him with every thrust. He buried his face in her neck, biting, sucking, marking her as his hips moved faster, chasing the sweet oblivion. Glen groaned as he sank deeper, the sensation of her wrapping around him stealing his breath. His urgency increased, hands gripping her thighs, pulling her hips up to meet every deep, unrelenting thrust.

Yolaine let out a sharp gasp, her fingers digging into his shoulders. "Goodness, Glen..."

Her moans and the way she clung to him sent him into a frenzy. He wanted to consume, unravel her completely, and ensure she never forgot this moment.

His mouth found her breasts again, his tongue flicking over her hardened peaks, making her shudder beneath him. Her nails raked through his hair, urging him on as pleasure coiled tightly inside her.

"You're getting better at this," she teased breathlessly, her voice breaking as he thrust deeper, harder.

"Then I think I'll show you how much I've picked up," he muttered low and rough, flipping her onto her belly before she could utter a word. The shift was swift and commanding. She scrambled to her hands and knees, hips arched high like she'd been here before and knew what was coming, her bottom bare and vulnerable, inner thighs glistening in the light. Her body, slick with want, trembled beneath him, breath jagged as she buried her face in the pillow. His presence loomed behind her, heat pouring off him, warming her back, the air heavy with their unspoken need.

The new angle opened her up, and Glen guided his hard, thick length into her, slow and steady. She wasn't just wet—she was drenched, her body parting for him as he slid in effortlessly. Each thrust wove them tighter, raw and all-consuming. His hands clamped her hips, rough and sure, dragging her back into him with a deliberate rhythm that stoked the heat between them. Yolaine's body reacted on its own, arching beneath him, straining to meet him halfway.

But Glen wasn't letting her rush it. He wanted her to feel every second, to draw it out until they could hardly breathe. He yanked her back with a firm grip, sinking deeper with a gravelly growl of satisfaction. Her breath caught, a soft moan spilling out as her core gripped him tight, trembling under his power.

Unable to resist, Glen landed a sharp spank on her bottom, the crack slicing through the room. Her body jolted, the sting igniting a blaze inside her. She gasped, fingers clawing the sheets, her core pulsing as pleasure crashed into pain. He leaned close, lips brushing her ear, voice low and thick with desire.

"You like that, don't you, love?" The hunger in his words sent shivers down her spine.

Yolaine moaned, heat flooding her as she shoved back against him, silently begging for more, deeper. She knew he'd keep going—he always did. Another spank cracked down harder, the sound ringing out as she cried, her body quaking with the sweet, sharp thrill.

"More," she whispered, voice ragged, the mix of him inside her and the sting of his hand pushing her wild.

Glen didn't falter. His thrusts turned fierce, pinning her deeper into the mattress, his hand smacking her bottom again, their rhythm a heady clash of pleasure and dominance.

"Goodness, Yolaine—you feel bloody amazing," he rasped, voice dripping with need. Her muffled moans against the pillow drove him on as he claimed her with a hunger that matched the storm raging inside them. "Tell me you're mine," he growled, breath scorching her neck.

"Yours—always," she gasped, lost in him, her body shaking as he pushed her further into ecstasy.

"Tell me you'll feed me whenever I'm hungry," Glen demanded, voice rough with a playful edge. Yolaine screamed out,

"Yes, I will—now stop talking, spank me more; I love this new you!" Glen obeyed, his hand cracking down again, firm and sure. With Pierce, she'd never been herself, but with Glen, she could let loose—her inner fire flaring wild in their bed, free and accurate.

"If you want to claim me, you need to fill me up," Yolaine cried, voice breaking with need.

"I will," he growled back, sliding inside her from behind, hands gripping her hips tighter. He moved slowly and hard, a rhythm that rocked her deep.

This side of Yolaine—untamed, moaning, begging—he'd never dared dream of it. He loved it, her moans and feeling like a man in command. His length filled her, stretching her, and with every thrust, he took her higher, their connection blazing fierce and unstoppable.

"I'm—, I'm close," he groaned, his grip tightening.

"Don't stop," she breathed, pushing back against him. "Come inside me."

That was all he needed. With a shuddering growl, he buried himself deep, pleasure tearing through him as he found his release. His body tensed, then melted into hers, the aftershocks leaving them both breathless and trembling.

They just lay there momentarily, tangled in sweat-slicked sheets, their bodies buzzing in the aftermath. But then—

A bell rang from outside.

Yolaine's eyes widened. "Shit—Grandma!"

Glen barely had time to react before they scrambled to get dressed, hands fumbling to cover the evidence of their morning sin.

Still breathless and flushed, Yolaine threw him a wicked grin as she pulled on her oversized t-shirt.

"Next time," she teased, "we might need to be quieter."

Glen smirked, pulling her close for one last lingering kiss.

"Not a chance."

Glen shoved the door open, his breath still ragged, his chest rising and falling as if he had sprinted a mile. Kaley wasted no time. She darted past him, her tiny feet pattering against the floor, her eager eyes sweeping the room until they landed on Yolaine.

Sprawled across the bed, she looked utterly undone. Her body melted into the sheets, limbs lax, her chest lifting in shallow, uneven breaths.

"Mama!" Kaley squealed, flinging herself onto the bed, her tiny hands gripping Yolaine's arm as she giggled. "You won't believe what I did with Great-Grandma today!"

Yolaine barely registered the words.

Her body still *thrummed*, aftershocks rippling through her in slow, insidious waves. Her skin felt *too sensitive*; every breath was an effort, and every movement was a reminder. *Deep inside*, where he had been only moments ago, the heat of him lingered—a trace of something forbidden, seeping, unignorable.

Her fingers curled into the sheets, desperate to tether herself back to reality, but it was futile.

*It was him.*

*My cousin.*

*The boy who became a man—the man who made me feel like a girl again. Like a teenager tangled in young, reckless passion. Like lovers hiding, sneaking, surrendering.*

*It was an experience I never had... until now.*

A shudder rolled through her as the weight of it settled—heavy, intoxicating, terrifying. She couldn't move. She *should* move.

Kaley tugged at her arm again, oblivious to the turmoil unravelling inside her mother.

"Mama?"

Yolaine inhaled sharply, forcing composure, forcing control. She smoothed a trembling hand over Kaley's hair, her fingers betraying her as they quivered against the soft strands.

"Go play in the living room, sweetheart," she murmured, her voice barely steady. "Mummy will be right there."

Kaley beamed, kissing her mother's cheek quickly before hopping off the bed and skipping away.

The door clicked shut.

Silence.

Yolaine exhaled, her body sinking *fully* into the mattress, no longer able to hold itself up.

She was in ecstasy.

Inside. Outside. Everywhere.

Her stomach clenched, her thighs pressed together in instinct, but it did nothing to stop the slow, *undeniable* warmth slipping between them.

She needed to move. To get up. To clean herself.

Beyond the bedroom, laughter echoed—light, unburdened. Glen and Grandma chatting as if the world hadn't just shifted. As if nothing had changed.

But Yolaine knew better.

Everything had changed.

Yolaine stepped out of the bathroom, feeling more relaxed and more composed. The warmth of the water had washed away the lingering tension in her muscles, but not the thoughts that swirled in her mind.

Walking into the living room, she spotted Grandma chatting with Glen while Kaley played on the floor, lost in her little world. Her gaze fell on Glen, and for a moment, doubt crept in. *Have I dragged him into something even more complicated?*

He had come to escape heartbreak and clear his mind, yet here she was, making things even messier. Maybe it was time to end this—to normalise their relationship, to pull away before it went too far.

But then she looked at him again. The way he laughed so quickly, his eyes lighting up, his grin boyish and carefree.

And she smiled.

*Fate brought us here to this exact moment. This wasn't supposed to happen... and yet, here we are.*

He had made her feel good—genuinely *alive*—in ways she hadn't in years. With him, she forgot the weight she had been carrying, the heartache she had endured. He made her feel like *herself* again.

She had given Pierce a second chance, even when she knew he hadn't changed deep down. She had stayed for Kaley's sake. But how long could she keep pretending?

No. She wouldn't let life pass her by anymore. She could be a good mother *and* still allow herself to *feel* again.

Yolaine took Glen and Kaley to Janice's mother's house that evening. Janice had invited them for dinner; for once, Yolaine didn't overthink things.

She was going to *live*.

Later that evening, Yolaine looked for Glen, finding him sprawled across her bed, fast asleep. His breathing was steady, arms folded beneath his head, looking far too comfortable for someone who was supposed to be getting ready.

She sighed, stepping closer. "Glen."

No response.

She nudged his shoulder. "Wake up. We're late already."

He groaned, burying his face into the pillow. "You go ahead. I'll stay back."

Yolaine folded her arms. "Not happening. Janice invited *us*—all of us. Get up."

Glen didn't budge.

Her patience snapped. She grabbed his wrist and yanked him up with surprising strength, nearly toppling him off the bed. "Move it."

Grumbling under his breath, he finally dragged himself to the bathroom. A few minutes later, he emerged, hair slightly damp, throwing on a casual t-shirt and jeans.

Yolaine gave him a once-over and rolled her eyes. "Honestly, boys will always be boys. Can't you at least *try* to dress properly?"

Kaley giggled from the doorway, pointing at Glen. "Mummy's scolding you."

Glen only smirked, stuffing his hands into his pockets. "Relax. I'm not meeting the Queen." Then, without waiting for a response, he strode past them towards the car.

Janice welcomed them at the door, ushering them inside with a warm smile. "Finally! Thought you lot got lost."

She introduced them to her mother, her husband, Martin, and their teenage daughter, Caro, before leading them to the dining area.

As the evening progressed, Yolaine couldn't help but notice how distant Glen remained. He kept to himself, hardly engaging in conversation, choosing instead to sit with Kaley, keeping her entertained. He wasn't rude—just detached.

Janice leaned in close to Yolaine, lowering her voice. "He's not much of a talker, is he?"

Yolaine gave a small smile. "He's a reserved guy. It takes time to warm up to people."

Janice smirked knowingly. "Hmm. And why exactly is he here with you?"

Yolaine hesitated. But Janice had that look, which meant she wasn't letting this go.

Sighing, she relented. "He had a bad breakup. Came here to clear his head."

Janice's smirk widened. "Ah. So, *he's* the heartbroken one, and *you* are—" She trailed off before chuckling. "This sounds *very* familiar."

Yolaine narrowed her eyes. "Don't start."

Janice laughed, a hint of mischief in her tone. "Oh, darling, I'm *just* saying—be careful. Wouldn't want history repeating itself, would we?"

Yolaine forced a smile, but something about Janice's words gnawed at her.

Throughout dinner, Janice's eyes flicked between Glen and Yolaine as if searching for unspoken truth. She grew bolder, testing the waters. She draped her arm casually over Glen's shoulder, let her fingers graze his arm a little longer than necessary, and even rested a hand briefly on his thigh during the conversation.

Yolaine watched.

Glen, however, barely reacted. If he noticed, he didn't show it. To him, Janice was nothing more than Yolaine's old friend. Nothing more.

But Yolaine knew better.

Janice wasn't just being friendly—she was *testing* him.

*Testing them.*

And she wasn't about to let Janice play games she had no business playing.

As soon as dinner ended, Yolaine stood. "We should head back. Grandma's alone, and it's getting late."

Janice tilted her head, amused. "That eager to leave?"

Yolaine smiled, but there was an edge to it. "We'll catch up soon."

She didn't miss the way Janice's eyes lingered on Glen one last time before they left.

Back home, Kaley was tucked into bed, drifting into a peaceful slumber. Grandma had already retired for the night.

Yolaine stepped outside, finding Glen sitting on the porch, one leg stretched out, the other bent, an unreadable expression on his face. The air was thick with the scent of damp earth, a cool breeze sweeping through the night.

Without a word, she sat beside him.

Silence stretched between them, comfortable yet charged. The events of the evening replayed in her mind.

After a long pause, she finally spoke. "You noticed what she was doing, didn't you?"

Glen exhaled through his nose, a ghost of a smile tugging at his lips. "She wasn't exactly subtle."

Yolaine turned to him, watching his profile in the dim light. "Didn't bother you?"

He glanced at her then, his gaze steady, unreadable. "Should it have?"

Glen looked at Yolaine, his gaze steady yet unreadable. Slowly, he reached out, his warm hand covering hers. Their eyes met—neither speaking nor understanding.

The air between them felt thick, charged with something neither wanted to name.

Yolaine hesitated and then spoke, her voice softer than she intended. "Pierce messaged me... asking when I'd be coming back."

She paused, searching Glen's face for a reaction. "I haven't responded yet. I'd rather stay here a while longer—it's peaceful."

Glen didn't say a word. His grip on her hand didn't tighten or pull away. He remained still, unreadable.

Yolaine studied him, feeling the weight of his silence. Then, gently, she laced her fingers through his, her touch deliberate. "Come on," she murmured, standing up and tugging him along. "It's been a long day. Let's get some rest."

She led him inside, her hand still in his.

Glen followed without resistance, though his mind was a storm of thoughts he dared not voice.

Once inside, he quietly prepared his makeshift bed in the living room while Yolaine disappeared into the bathroom to freshen up. A few minutes later, she slipped into bed beside Kaley, the little girl already lost in dreams.

The house settled into silence.

The night stretched on, thick with silence yet heavy with unspoken desire.

Yolaine lay on her side, the cool sheets tangled around her restless body. Sleep evaded her, refusing to come. Her skin burned, her mind raced, her body hummed with the ache of unfinished need.

And she knew why.

He was there across the house, not far from where she lay.

She could feel it—his presence, his heat, the slow, steady rhythm of his breath. It pulled at her like a magnetic force, an invisible thread binding them together in the dark.

She wanted to go to him.

She wanted to slip out of bed, feel his warmth, and let his strong arms envelop her. His touch reminded her of everything she had been craving.

But she hesitated.

Glen had been through enough. He may need time and space. Perhaps she was selfish, wanting more of him when he should be resting.

Yolaine exhaled slowly, shutting her eyes, forcing herself to surrender to the night, to forget the pulsing ache between her thighs.

But then—a shift.

A presence.

A warmth pressed against her back.

And then, a touch.

Firm hands slipped around her waist, pulling her in, claiming her. The heat of his palm flattened against her stomach, his fingers spreading, possessive, commanding.

Her breath hitched.

The scent of him—warm, masculine, intoxicating—enveloped her, and she knew.

He had come to her.

Her lips parted, but before she could speak, she felt it—his lips grazing the nape of her neck, warm, soft, teasing.

A delicious shiver rippled through her body.

Glen exhaled against her skin, his breath heavy, ragged, filled with a hunger she knew all too well.

She tilted her head, giving him silent permission. Her fingers reached back, tangling in his thick hair and pulling him closer.

A low groan rumbled from his throat.

His mouth trailed down her shoulder, his tongue flicking against the delicate skin, igniting a fire deep within her.

His hand moved lower, gliding over the curve of her hip, exploring and teasing as his fingertips traced the hem of her nightdress.

Yolaine gasped softly as he slipped beneath it, fingertips skimming the sensitive skin of her inner thighs.

She was already wet. Glen felt it, too.

A deep, satisfied chuckle vibrated against her neck.

"Missed me, love?" he murmured, his voice thick with amusement and something darker, something primal.

She didn't answer—not with words.

Instead, she arched against him, pressing her hips back, feeling the undeniable hardness of him pressing against her, thick and rigid.

He groaned, his grip tightening on her hip.

His fingers dipped between her folds, spreading her slickness, teasing her with slow, torturous strokes.

Yolaine let out a muffled moan, biting her lip, her body trembling beneath his touch.

Kaley was asleep beside her.

They had to be quiet. But Glen was wicked.

He pushed the fabric of her nightdress higher, exposing her completely to him.

Her breath hitched as he eased his thick shaft against her, rubbing, teasing, coating himself in her wetness.

Yolaine spooned against him, parting her thighs slightly, granting him better access.

He didn't rush.

Instead, he took his time, pressing the thick head of his shaft against her entrance from behind, teasing her, pushing just enough to make her gasp with anticipation.

Then—he thrust, slow and deep.

Her inner walls clenched around him, pulling him in, welcoming, consuming him.

His size stretched her deliciously, filling her inch by inch until he was buried entirely within her heat.

A shuddered breath escaped Yolaine's lips.

She reached behind, gripping his hip, urging him to move.

He obeyed.

His rhythm was slow, deep, and deliberate.

Every thrust sent a ripple of pleasure coursing through her; every roll of his hips made her body tighten with need.

He was taking his time, savouring every second, every squeeze of her warmth around him.

She gasped when his hand slid over her thigh, gripping the back of her knee, lifting it slightly to allow him to sink even more profoundly.

Her moans were quiet, breathless, a symphony only he could hear.

"You're a devil," she whispered, her voice trembling with pleasure.

Glen let out a low, wicked chuckle, his teeth grazing her earlobe.

"And you, love... are my dream."

A shudder ran through her.

His thrusts quickened slightly, his grip tightening as he drove into her with slow, precise strokes, each one sending her higher, pushing her closer to the edge.

She buried her face into the pillow, her fingers gripping the sheets, her body quaking, her breath ragged.

Glen wrapped an arm around her waist, holding her firmly against him as he brought her to the brink.

The room was bathed in soft, dim light, their whispered breaths the only sound in the stillness.

Yolaine's body tensed, her back arching as the pleasure crashed over her in waves, her walls pulsing, milking him.

Glen groaned, his grip tightening as he thrust one last time, burying himself to the hilt, his release shuddering through him.

For a moment, neither of them moved.

They lay there, entangled, breathless, their bodies still joined, trembling from the aftershocks of pleasure.

Yolaine sighed, a lazy, satisfied smile curving her lips.

Glen kissed her shoulder, his breath still warm against her skin.

"We should sleep," he murmured, though neither of them made a move to part.

Yolaine only hummed, pulling his arm tighter around her waist.

Let the world wait.

They lay there, caught in the haze of satisfaction, bodies still thrumming with the aftershocks of pleasure. Glen's arm was wrapped around Yolaine's waist, his hold firm, possessive. She could feel his breath against her neck, warm, steady, grounding her. His heartbeat was a deep, rhythmic pulse against her spine, a reminder that this wasn't a dream.

Yolaine traced slow circles over his forearm, her fingers lazy, her mind blissfully clouded. She had craved this: to be wanted, worshipped, and feel like more than just a woman, but a force, an ache, a hunger that couldn't be denied. Yet, despite the pleasure in her veins, the fire inside her refused to die.

She wanted more.

Turning in his arms, she met his gaze in the dim glow of the bedside lamp. Her fingers brushed over the sharp lines of his jaw, trailing down to his lips, swollen from their kisses. Slowly, she leaned in, her mouth capturing his in a deep, languid, teasing kiss.

Glen groaned against her lips, his grip on her waist tightening.

"I want more," she whispered, her breath a hot caress against his mouth. "Can you give me more?"

A slow smirk tugged at his lips, but his eyes burned with the same hunger that set her ablaze.

And here I thought you were spent," he murmured, his voice thick. His fingers trailed down her back, teasing, possessive. "But if you're asking—"

She silenced him with another kiss, deeper this time, dragging her nails down his chest. But reality intruded—the bed was too small, the air too still. And just inches away, Kaley was sleeping, completely unaware of the forbidden hunger crackling between them.

Yolaine pulled away, breathless, a knowing smile playing on her lips.

Wordlessly, she reached for the clothes scattered around them—not to put on but to carry along to the living room. Glen followed suit, gathering his jeans and shirt, a wicked gleam in his eyes as he intertwined his fingers with hers. They moved in silence, their bare bodies illuminated by the soft flicker of light spilling from the hallway as they slipped out of the room.

Their steps were light and careful, yet the air around them was electric. Every heartbeat, breath, and skin brush against skin whispered what was coming.

The living room was dim, bathed in the golden glow of the city lights filtering through the curtains. The makeshift bed—blankets and cushions spread over the floor—waited for them like a promise.

Yolaine turned to face him, her bare body pressing flush against his. The air between them sizzled as she tilted her chin up, meeting his gaze with a smirk.

"Now," she murmured, her lips grazing his, "let's see if you can keep up."

Before he could respond, she pushed him back against the nearest wall, her body moulding against his as she claimed his lips again—fierce, desperate, insatiable. Glen groaned, his hands roaming, gripping, rediscovering her curves like he was carving them into his memory.

His control snapped.

With a growl, he lifted her, carrying her to the makeshift bed in swift, confident strides before lowering her onto the cushions. But the moment he joined her, there was no patience, no hesitation.

His mouth found hers, then her jaw, then lower—trailing down her throat, across the slope of her breast, worshipping her with slow, open-mouthed kisses that made her shudder beneath him. His hands followed, kneading, exploring, teasing until she was writhing, gasping, her fingers tangling in his hair, urging him lower.

She let out a sharp gasp when his lips found the soft skin of her inner thigh, his breath a whisper against her heat. He lingered there, kissing, teasing, his tongue barely grazing her folds before retreating, dragging a frustrated moan from her lips.

He smirked against her skin. "I could stay here all night."

Yolaine let out a breathless laugh, threading her fingers through his hair. "Whose stopping you," she murmured, her voice dripping with promise. Then, with a teasing roll of her hips, she shifted back, slipping from his grasp, leaving him wanting.

His eyes darkened, but she only smirked.

Yolaine straddled him, settling herself just above where he ached for her the most. She moved deliberately, rolling her hips in slow, teasing motions, letting the thick length of his press against her without giving in just yet. Glen groaned, his fingers gripping her thighs, his restraint unravelling with every taunting shift of her body.

A wicked smile played on her lips as she leaned forward, pressing her chest against his, her breath warm against his jaw. "Patience," she whispered, revelling in the way his muscles tensed beneath her.

Glen's fingers tightened on her hips, his restraint hanging by a thread. "Yolaine," he rasped, his voice thick with desperation.

She leaned in, her breath hot against his ear. "Just hold on tight."

With aching slowness, she reached between them, wrapping her fingers around his thick shaft. Guiding him between her folds, she let the tip press against her entrance, feeling the anticipation coil tight in her belly. Then, inch by inch, she sank onto him, her body stretching, adjusting, taking him in until he was utterly sheathed within her.

A shudder wracked her as she felt him fill her, the deep pressure both overwhelming and exquisite. Her walls fluttered around him, savouring the sweet ache of being so wholly claimed. Glen groaned, his head falling back, his grip on her hips tightening as if he needed to ground himself in the moment.

Yolaine exhaled a shaky breath, adjusting to the fullness and intensity. She had him now—completely, utterly. And now, it was her turn to take control.

A shuddering breath tore from Glen's lips, his hands gripping her thighs as his head fell back against the cushions.

"Goodness," he groaned, his voice breaking.

A wicked smile played on her lips. "Then hold on tight, love."

She set the rhythm, slow and hypnotic, her body moving with a grace that made his control unravel. Every roll of her hips was a promise, every moan a plea, every gasp a surrender. Glen's hands guided her, gripping, kneading, worshipping.

Faster. Deeper.

The pleasure coiled between them, tightening, spiralling, building into something uncontrollable, something that threatened to consume them both.

Glen's grip on her thighs tightened, his breath ragged.

"I'm close," he groaned, his voice breaking.

Yolaine leaned down, her lips brushing against his ear, her voice dripping with seduction.

"Let it go, sweetheart. Give it to me."

And he did.

A strangled moan tore from his throat as his release crashed over him, his body tensing, shuddering beneath her. Hot fluid gushed into her, and she could feel every pulse, every throbbing wave of his pleasure spilling deep inside. But Yolaine didn't stop—she rode him through it, drawing out every last drop, pushing him until there was nothing left to give until he was utterly spent beneath her.

Only when she felt her pleasure crest—blinding, all-consuming—did she finally collapse against him, her body trembling, her breath coming in short, uneven gasps.

She let out a breathless chuckle, trailing her fingers lazily over his chest. "Not bad... this is the second time you came into me in one night."

Still catching his breath, Glen blushed slightly before a slow grin spread across his face. "Well, you're hot... and you have a way of bringing out the best in me."

For a long moment, the only sound was their breathing, their bodies still tangled in the remnants of their passion.

Glen's hands roamed her back in slow, lazy strokes, his lips pressing against her temple.

"You," he murmured, his voice thick with exhaustion and satisfaction, "are going to be the death of me."

Yolaine grinned, her lips ghosting over his damp skin.

"Then what a way to go."

Yolaine slid away on the bed, her body still warm from their shared passion. Glen exhaled deeply, running a hand through his tousled hair before quietly excusing himself. He reached for his half-pants, slipping them on before going to the bathroom to wash up. The cool water against his skin did little to chase away the heat lingering in his veins.

When Glen returned to the living room, Yolaine was nowhere to be found. He sank into the couch, the room's silence filling him with a strange emptiness as he waited for her return. There she was—Yolaine, dressed in her nightgown, as graceful as ever, returning to the living room. She held a container of ice cream piled high in her hands, a playful smile tugging at her lips.

"I'm feeling hot," she said lightly, her voice carefree and light. "Felt like having ice cream."

Glen raised an eyebrow, his lips curling into a grin. "It's almost 3 a.m., and you want ice cream?"

Yolaine's eyes sparkled mischievously. "When I'm excited, I love to eat," she winked at him as if her reasoning was all the explanation he needed.

Glen chuckled, the sound warm and familiar. "Now you're talking." Without hesitation, he slipped into his shorts and joined her on the couch. Glen couldn't help but notice the subtle shift in the air as they dug into the ice cream.

Glen couldn't shake the feeling that something had changed as they sat together. Yolaine, his older cousin, had always been beautiful, but tonight, there was something different about her. She seemed to radiate an effortless elegance that left him momentarily speechless. She looked stunning—almost ethereal. Her slender frame, untouched by time, was a quiet reminder that she had lived a whole life, one that most would never guess by just looking at her. No one would believe she was a married woman, a mother. She carried herself so gracefully, so timelessly, it was as though she had never aged.

They had grown up together—mischievous children, teasing and playing with each other, never thinking beyond the innocence of their shared childhood. But now, as they sat side by side in the quiet of the night, there was something unspoken between them. Glen's gaze lingered a little longer than it should have, drawn to how the years had been so kind to her. She was still the girl he remembered, but somehow, she had become someone else—someone he couldn't quite place.

A boy had once entered her life, and Yolaine had turned him into a man. The thought sent a shiver down Glen's spine. The weight of that realisation hung heavy between them, a tension neither could ignore. They weren't just cousins anymore. The distance between them had grown in time, and how they now saw each other. For a moment, Glen was caught between the familiarity of their childhood and the undeniable shift that had taken place. Something had changed, and neither of them could pretend it hadn't.

"Hello, where're you at? Why're you so quiet?" Yolaine murmured, her voice a soft, teasing caress as she tilted her head, eyes glinting with playful curiosity. Glen didn't answer immediately—just gave a faint nod, a spark of something tender flickering in his gaze. "Nothing, really," he replied at last, his tone hushed, almost reverent, like he was guarding a secret meant only for her ears. He looked at her—honestly looked—his eyes tracing the gentle curve of her face with a quiet, aching adoration. Reaching out, he eased the ice cream tub from her hands, setting it aside as if it dared intrude on their moment. Then he leaned in, his lips grazing hers in a tender, hesitant kiss, a question hanging in the air. She didn't pull back—she melted into him, her breath hitching as their kiss unfurled into something deeper, richer, a sweet collision of longing.

They sank into one another, hands roaming to familiar havens, lips moving with a slow, deliberate hunger. It was the third time that night they'd fallen into this intoxicating dance, yet each kiss felt like a fresh vow, each touch a velvet whisper of devotion.

"Where're you heading with this?" she grinned, a knowing spark in her eyes—she could guess his next move.

Glen's lips curved into a sly smile. "I can take it, love—want you more," he rasped, his voice thick with need. He left her lips, trailing scorching kisses down her neck, his hands gliding to her breasts, teasing her with slow, deliberate caresses. With a gentle tug, he slipped her nightdress over her shoulders, letting it fall away, baring her to his gaze. He kissed her breasts, soft and reverent, then suckled her nipples, drawing them into tight peaks. She pulled him closer, pressing his face deeper into her chest, a moan spilling from her lips—she knew he craved her, and this raw, new hunger in him was something she wouldn't halt.

His hands roamed her body, slow and exploratory, fingers brushing her inner thighs, feeling the soft folds of her skin. She parted her legs, a silent invitation, granting him more access as her breath quickened. He slid down, burying his face in her inner thighs, the heat of his breath sending shivers through her. She pushed him deeper, urging him on, and he kissed her folds, his tongue delving slow and deep, tasting her with a lover's care.

"Glen, don't stop," she pleaded, her voice trembling. He didn't—sucking and teasing her with relentless focus, he slipped a finger inside, curling it as he lapped at her, drawing out her pleasure. She spread her legs, quivering excitedly, and a soft scream broke free.

"Glen, I'm coming—don't stop!" she gasped, her body taut as he licked and sucked her folds, pushing her over the edge. She came, her body shivering with ecstatic release, collapsing back onto the pillow as she tugged him up.

"Take me, please," she breathed, her voice raw with need.

Still, on the couch, Yolaine sat upright, her legs splayed wide in a bold, unguarded invitation. Her hand found Glen's length—hard, thick, and ready, pulsing with a need that mirrored her own. She guided him inside her, pulling him close with a gentle tug, and he bent over her, sinking deep into her folds with a slow, deliberate thrust that stretched her exquisitely. A moan tore from her lips, raw and unrestrained, reverberating through the quiet room as her warmth enveloped him. Glen couldn't hold back—slipping deeper, he began to slide in and out, her legs wrapping around his hips, locking him tight against her. The rhythm started slow, a tender exploration, then surged into something faster, fiercer—an intense, primal union that consumed them both, a tempest of flesh and desire.

He moved with her like there was no tomorrow as if the night was theirs alone to claim. His hunger was ravenous—he wanted all of her, every inch, every shudder, tonight and tonight only. He took his time, savouring her feel, each thrust a deliberate act of worship, but the fire seething within him was too wild to tame. He couldn't control himself, the need overwhelming, his breaths coming in jagged gasps as he lost himself in her. "I'm coming," Glen whispered, his voice a ragged, desperate cry, trembling with the edge of release.

"Don't stop," she urged, her fingers digging into his shoulders, clinging to him as if he were her anchor. He came into her, his heat flooding through her for the third time that night—a scorching tide that bound them together, a molten thread tying their souls in that breathless, eternal moment. They froze, locked in that position, hearts hammering, unwilling to let the intimacy fracture.

After a lingering pause, Glen eased back onto the couch beside her, their eyes catching in the dim light—a shared, sated glow shimmering between them. They grinned, a flicker of mischief dancing in their gazes.

"That's the third time you've come into me tonight," she teased, her voice warm and playful, laced with a tender edge as she nudged him. "You've got some stamina, haven't you?" He chuckled, gently brushing a damp strand of hair from her face, his fingers lingering against her skin.

"It's you, sweetheart—you bring the beast out of me," he murmured, his tone soft yet brimming with adoration, a confession wrapped in a lover's sigh. Utterly spent, they shifted to the makeshift bed in the living room, too exhausted to venture further. The moment their heads sank into the pillows, sleep claimed them—a tender, tangled embrace swallowing them whole as the rain's distant roar faded into the velvet hush of the night.

As the first light of dawn crept into the room, Yolaine stirred, blinking against the soft golden glow. Then, realisation struck like a bolt of lightning. Her eyes darted around, taking in the sight—Glen, lying bare beside her, his chest rising and falling asleep. She gasped, jolting upright.

Heart racing, she grabbed her nightdress and slipped it on before giving Glen a sharp kick under the covers.

"Wake up," she hissed in a whisper.

Glen groaned, grumbling as he cracked open an eye. "What now?" he muttered sleepily.

"Get dressed," she ordered, her voice low but urgent.

Sighing, he sat up sluggishly, rubbing his face before dragging his clothes on. But the moment he was dressed, he flopped back onto the bed with a yawn instead of getting up.

Rolling her eyes, Yolaine left him and tiptoed back to her bedroom, slipping into bed beside Kaley. Her heart pounded with unease as she lay there, staring at the ceiling. Their little honeymoon period was about to be cut short.

Because what she didn't know—neither of them knew—was that Pierce was already on his way to take her back home.

#3
# Fated In The Stars

Yolaine was the first to wake, slipping out of bed to get Kaley washed and dressed for breakfast. In the kitchen, Grandma sat doting on Kaley, fussing over her like she was the most precious thing in the world.

Meanwhile, Yolaine returned to Glen's room and nudged him awake. He groaned, stretching lazily before catching her wrist and pulling her down onto the bed. Before she could protest, his lips were in a slow, teasing kiss.

She pushed at his chest. "Glen, please. We need to be careful."

With a reluctant sigh, he loosened his grip, and she slipped away, heading for the bathroom. But just as she turned on the tap, Glen appeared in the doorway, eyes gleaming with mischief.

She gasped. "Are you mad?" She tried to shove him away, but he held firm, a cheeky grin on his lips.

"Kaley and Grandma are busy in the kitchen," he whispered. "No one will notice if we're missing." His hands slid over her waist. "Come on, I'm having a hangover from you. Just a quick one."

Yolaine's pulse quickened, but she turned away, shaking her head. With one last warning glance, she slipped past him and peered into the kitchen. Kaley was munching away happily, and Grandma was far too busy pampering her to notice anything amiss.

Heart pounding, Yolaine made a split-second decision. She retraced her steps, slipping back into the bathroom where Glen stood waiting, his eyes alight with anticipation. When she shut the door behind her, he pounced, his hands greedily pulling at the oversized T-shirt she wore, dragging it over her head. She let out a breathless laugh, swatting at his chest, but he was not stopping now.

Her panties were next, pooling at her feet as he discarded his clothes. The water cascaded over them as they stepped into the shower, steam curling around their tangled bodies. Glen's hands roamed her slick skin, exploring every inch, his touch igniting fresh shivers down her spine.

He smirked, voice husky. "Now, this is something. A bath with my beautiful cousin—who would have thought?"

She hushed him with a sharp look, pressing a finger to his lips. "Lower your voice, you idiot."

But she was revelling in it—the thrill of sneaking around, the danger of getting caught, the way it made her feel alive. She craved this reckless indulgence, a wicked little game played at the edge of disaster.

She grasped his head, guiding him lower, her fingers threading through his damp hair. He immediately understood, his mouth trailing down, tasting and teasing her. When he finally reached her breasts, she sighed, arching into him as he took a nipple into his mouth, sucking greedily while rolling the other between his fingers.

Her breath hitched. "Lower," she murmured, pushing his head downward.

Glen grinned but obeyed, his mouth finding hers in a searing kiss. His hands trailed down her waist, slipping between her thighs. He knelt before her, his breath warm against her sensitive skin, and she parted her legs slightly in anticipation.

He kissed her inner thigh first, his lips trailing dangerously close before he finally pressed his mouth against her folds. A deep moan escaped her as his tongue flicked out, teasing, tasting.

Yolaine's hands tangled in his wet hair, gripping tightly as she rocked against his mouth. He licked her slowly, savouring every gasp and tremor, his tongue slipping deeper, pressing into her wet heat. She shivered as he rubbed his face against her, the light scrape of his stubble adding to the overwhelming sensation.

She arched her back, lifting one leg and resting it on his shoulder, giving him better access. Glen groaned against her, the vibration making her whimper. He delved deeper, his tongue stroking her inner walls, swirling and pressing as he feasted on her.

She felt his hands tighten on her thighs, spreading her even more expansive. Then, as if he needed to take her even further, he slid a finger inside her, thrusting slowly as his tongue continued its relentless assault.

Her body trembled violently, pleasure crashing over her like the rushing water around them. "Goodness, Glen," she whimpered, her head falling back against the tiles.

Glen groaned, pushing deeper, his tongue and finger working together to drive her mad. Yolaine's hips bucked, her breath coming in short, desperate gasps. She dug her nails into his shoulders, her body shuddering as the pleasure built to an unbearable peak.

She couldn't take it anymore. Tugging at his hair, she pulled him up to his feet, her lips crashing into his, tasting herself in his mouth.

"It's time," she whispered breathlessly.

He was more than ready, his hard, throbbing length pressing against her thigh. With one swift move, he lifted one of her legs and positioned himself at her entrance. A shudder passed through her as he pushed inside, her wetness guiding him in with ease.

Glen groaned, pressing himself deeper, his grip on her tightening as he moved—slow at first, then with increasing urgency, the intensity mounting between them. She clung to him, her nails sinking into his shoulders, the sensation of his thick, rigid length stretching her almost unbearable. He was larger than what she was used to—perhaps because he was young, brimming with vigour, his body thrumming with raw energy. To him, this was more than just passion; it was an exhilarating adventure, each thrust fuelled by unrestrained desire, his heat surging through her as he drove deeper, lost in the moment.

They devoured each other with reckless hunger as if it were their first time all over again. It didn't feel like just last night; they had taken and tasted everything the other had to offer.

"I can't hold it," Glen groaned, his voice raw, strained.

Yolaine tightened around him, her lips brushing against his ear. "Then don't."

He thrust into her, his movements growing frenzied, desperate. The tension coiled tighter and tighter, winding to the point of no return.

With a strangled moan, he gave in—his body shuddering as waves of hot, thick release spilt into her. His grip on her tightened as if anchoring himself to the sensation, refusing to let go even as his body pulsed with the aftershocks of pleasure.

Yolaine let out a breathless laugh, her own body still trembling. "Goodness, Glen," she teased between gasps, "you're like an endless supply of cream."

He smirked, utterly spent but still fixated on her.

She stepped out of the shower, the cool air shocking against her heated skin. She knew she had already taken a risk being here, but before she could wrap herself in a towel, Glen's hands were on her again—strong, relentless.

She twisted in his grasp. "Enough, Glen."

But he wasn't listening. He couldn't. His hunger for her was insatiable, a wildfire that refused to be extinguished. He had seen and heard things his entire life—but now he was feeling and *living* them. And he wanted more.

His hands found hers, guiding them back to his length—still impossibly hard, still pulsing with need. Yolaine hesitated but then curled her fingers around him, stroking slow, teasing. Glen groaned, his head falling back against the tiles, his body tightening like a drawn bow.

Then, in one swift motion, he spun her around, pressing her palms flat against the shower wall. She let out a sharp gasp as he entered her from behind, inch by inch, stretching her, filling her.

She didn't resist. She *couldn't*. She pushed back against him, matching his rhythm, surrendering to the heat pooling deep in her core. His grip on her hips was bruising, his thrusts deep and demanding, sending shockwaves of pleasure through every inch of her body.

Her teeth sank into her lip to silence the moan threatening to escape. But Glen wanted to hear her and listen to every sound she made. His hands slid up her body, finding her breasts, his fingers rolling and twisting her nipples as he drove into her from behind.

Her breath hitched. A shudder wrecked through her as the pleasure built unbearably fast.

This time, they unravelled together—her walls tightening around him, pulling him deeper as he groaned against her skin. But Glen had already spilt so much before; there was nothing left to give—only the raw, shuddering tremors of release that left them both weak and breathless.

Yolaine turned to face him, capturing his lips in a lingering, searing kiss before she pulled away. She stepped out of the shower, reaching for a towel, slipping on an oversized T-shirt as her body tingled with the aftermath.

Glen watched her go, still standing beneath the warm spray, his body exhausted yet craving her.

She didn't look back as she disappeared into her bedroom.

But they both knew—this wasn't over. Not yet.

She barely had time to steady herself before an excited little voice rang through the room.

"Daddy! Daddy!" Kaley squealed, leaping off her chair.

Yolaine's stomach twisted.

Pierce.

He stood in the doorway, smiling, his eyes warm as he saw their daughter.

Grandma beamed. "Surprise, love. He wanted to come and fetch you himself."

Yolaine forced a smile, her heart pounding as Pierce stepped closer.

Then, just as she feared, Glen emerged from the hallway. His hair was still damp, his shirt clinging to his skin, and the remnants of their encounter lingering on him. His gaze flickered between Yolaine and the man now standing before her.

Yolaine swallowed hard, her throat dry. "Pierce, this is Glen—my cousin."

Pierce turned to him, extending a hand. "Ah, I remember him. Last time I saw you, you were just a kid."

Glen hesitated, only for a fraction of a second, before clasping the offered hand. "Hi," he murmured, his voice measured.

As Pierce turned back to Kaley, distracted by her excited chatter, Glen quietly moved to the sofa and sank onto it, shoulders tense. His pulse thundered in his ears.

Less than an hour ago, he had been buried inside Yolaine.

And now her husband was standing right there.

The game had just taken a dangerous new turn.

#4

# Boundaries and Curves

Dinner was a quiet affair, filled with forced smiles and hollow conversation. Pierce had slipped back into place seamlessly, as though he had never left. He belonged here—at the head of the table, at Yolaine's side, basking in their daughter's affection. His presence was steady, warm, and undeniably familiar.

And suffocating.

Glen barely spoke. He pushed his food around his plate; muscles wound tight beneath his skin. Across from him, Yolaine played her role flawlessly—nodding at the right moments, smiling on cue, and laughing light and convincingly. But beneath it all, her nerves were frayed, her body still tingling with the ghost of Glen's touch, and his imprint burned into her skin.

Pierce's attention never strayed from Kaley, who was drinking in her excitement with the kind of devotion only a father could give. She beamed at him, filling the space with innocent joy neither Yolaine nor Glen could partake in. It was a cruel irony—her happiness only magnified Yolaine's turmoil and deepened Glen's frustration.

After dinner, Pierce leaned back in his chair, stretching. "I'll put Kaley to bed," he said, scooping their daughter up effortlessly before she could protest.

Yolaine barely heard him. Across the room, Glen stood near the window, bathed in the dim evening light. His hands were shoved into his pockets, his shoulders tense, and his jaw set. He had barely looked at her since Pierce walked through the door.

Pierce turned to Glen, clapping him on the shoulder. "You'll be alright in the living room, won't you?"

Glen forced a smile, nodding. "Yeah, no problem."

Pierce chuckled, oblivious to the silent current of tension. "Good man." With that, he disappeared down the hall, Kaley's sleepy giggles fading behind him.

The moment the door clicked shut, the air shifted. Heavy. Charged.

Yolaine turned to Glen. Their eyes met for the first time since the intrusion of reality, and in that instant, the restraint shattered. The heat, the longing, the raw ache that had been simmering between them all day roared back to life. But now, there was something else—denial, restraint, a maddening awareness of the boundary neither could cross tonight.

Neither of them spoke.

Yolaine opened her mouth, desperate to say something, anything, to ease the torment tightening her chest. But the words caught in her throat, strangled by everything left unsaid. Glen's lips curled into a bitter smirk, his eyes dark, resigned. He grabbed the spare blanket from the couch and tossed it onto the makeshift bed on the floor.

"Goodnight," he muttered, turning away.

Yolaine exhaled shakily, forcing herself to move and walk toward the bedroom where Pierce lay waiting. Every step felt like a betrayal. Her mind screamed at her to turn back, to stay, but she didn't.

She pushed the door open, slipping inside without another glance at Glen.

Pierce was already settled beneath the covers, and Kaley nestled against him. He smiled sleepily, patting the space beside him. "Come to bed," he murmured, voice low and drowsy.

Yolaine hesitated, just for a moment.

Then she slid beneath the sheets, lying stiffly beside him. Pierce drifted off within minutes, his breathing deep and even. But she remained awake, staring at the ceiling, her mind a battlefield of guilt and desire.

Glen was just beyond that door. Alone. Awake.

She squeezed her eyes shut, willing herself to ignore the magnetic pull between them, the ache that stretched across the walls separating them.

Glen stared at the ceiling in the living room, frustration burning through his veins. His fists clenched beneath the blanket, his body aching for what he couldn't have tonight. What had been stolen from him the moment Pierce walked through that door?

The first night apart was unbearable.

And it was only the beginning.

The morning air was thick with unspoken words. The clatter of dishes and the occasional scrape of cutlery against plates were the only sounds filling the breakfast table.

Pierce sat at the head, sipping his coffee, his posture relaxed, his expression unreadable. Oblivious to the tension, Kaley chattered away about how she wanted to go to the park later. Grandma nodded along, beaming at her granddaughter's excitement.

Yolaine barely touched her food. Glen was even worse, merely stirring his coffee, his gaze fixed on the table. He hadn't looked at her once since they sat down. The weight of the previous night lingered in the air, pressing down on them.

Pierce's voice cut through the silence. "I was thinking we could all go out for lunch today. Maybe take a walk around town and let Kaley have some fun.

It's been a while since we've done something as a family." His smile was easy, almost too easy.

Yolaine forced a nod, her stomach twisting. "That sounds nice."

Glen finally looked up, his expression carefully neutral. "Yeah, sure."

Pierce gave him an approving nod as if he were pleased that Glen was willing to go along with the plan. "Great. It'll be good for all of us."

Yolaine felt Glen's gaze on her for just a second before he looked away again, retreating into himself. She clenched her fork tighter, determined to be alone with him before they left.

The opportunity came minutes later when Glen stepped out into the hallway. Yolaine followed swiftly, her heart pounding.

"Hey," she said softly, touching his arm.

He turned to her, his jaw tight. "Yolaine—"

"How are you?" she asked, searching his eyes. "Please, don't let this get to you. Just stay calm. Nothing's changed between us."

Glen let out a dry chuckle, shaking his head. "I don't want to cause any problems between you and Pierce."

Yolaine stepped closer, lifting a hand to his face, her thumb grazing his cheek. "Don't worry. I'll handle this."

His lips parted slightly, but before he could respond, they heard footsteps approaching. Yolaine quickly dropped her hand and stepped back just as Pierce emerged from the kitchen.

"There you two are," he said smoothly. "Ready to go?"

Yolaine nodded, keeping her expression neutral. "Yeah, let's go."

Pierce's gaze flickered between them for a second before he smiled. "Perfect."

If Pierce suspected anything, he didn't show it. He played the role of the devoted father and doting husband effortlessly, keeping Yolaine close and keeping Kaley entertained. He was careful and calculated—never pressing, never questioning why Glen was there. But Yolaine could see it in his eyes. He was watching, waiting.

They walked around for quite a while before settling for lunch at a charming little café. While walking, he purposely held Yolaine's and Kaley's hands—like a statement, a silent claim. Yolaine knew precisely what he was doing.

Pierce made sure Yolaine's favourite dish was ordered at lunch without her even asking. He was attentive and affectionate but not overbearing. Glen, meanwhile, remained quiet, offering the occasional forced smile when necessary.

Grandma was delighted to have the family together and chattered away about everything and anything. If she noticed the tension, she didn't let it show.

By the time they returned home, the late afternoon had passed in a haze of forced smiles and carefully curated moments. Pierce had played his part well. Yolaine knew precisely what he was doing—winning Kaley's heart, reminding Yolaine of what they once had, subtly weaving himself back into her life.

And the worst part? He was good at it.

Pierce kept himself busy with Kaley, reading to her, playing with her, and laughing. It was a performance, and Yolaine knew it. He wasn't just being a good father—he was using Kaley as leverage, knowing she was Yolaine's weakness.

Outside, in the fading evening light, Yolaine sat with Grandma and Glen on the lawn, their conversation flowing. She included Glen, throwing him small glances, giving him subtle smiles, and reassuring him that he wasn't an outsider.

She saw how he looked at her when he thought no one else was watching. The longing. The frustration. The restraint.

And she felt it, too.

That night, as Yolaine slipped into bed, Pierce was already waiting. Kaley was asleep between them, her tiny breaths soft and steady.

Pierce turned onto his side, wrapping an arm around Yolaine's waist. She stiffened at the touch.

"I've missed this," he murmured, his breath warm against her skin.

She didn't respond.

His hand slid down, his fingers grazing her hip. She swallowed hard, closing her eyes. But when his touch grew bolder, she reached down and caught his wrist, stopping him.

Pierce stilled, his eyes searching hers in the dim light. Then, slowly, he exhaled and withdrew his hand, shifting onto his back.

"Goodnight, Yolaine," he said, his voice unreadable.

She turned onto her side, staring at the wall, her heart hammering.

In the living room, Glen lay awake, staring at the ceiling.

The game was still being played.

And the stakes were only getting higher.

The morning unfolded like any other. Breakfast was routine, conversation was minimal, and the underlying tension remained unspoken. But Glen needed to clear his head. The weight of the past few days was suffocating, and the house—charged with emotions he wasn't ready to confront—was the last place he wanted to be.

He took off on his bike, the wind biting against his skin as he sped through the familiar streets. He hadn't planned for any of this. He'd come here to escape his heartache and find some clarity; instead, he'd been tangled in something far more complicated—something he hadn't been prepared for.

Meanwhile, Yolaine felt his absence at home more than she cared to admit. She forced herself to appear unaffected, going about her day as though it didn't matter. But it did. He hadn't returned for lunch; by early evening, the restlessness had settled deep within her bones.

When Glen finally walked through the door, his hair windswept, his clothes carrying the scent of the day's adventures, Yolaine didn't hesitate. She met him head-on, no longer concerned whether Pierce noticed or not.

"You need to freshen up," she said, her voice firm, leaving no room for argument. "We're going out."

Glen frowned. "Where?"

"Janice's. We're staying the night."

That caught him off guard. He hadn't expected to be back at Janice's so soon. They'd just visited the other day. But he didn't question it. He nodded, heading off to shower and change.

Yolaine had already informed Pierce of her plans. She told him she'd stay overnight at Janice's, and he hadn't protested. He was too calculated for that. He knew his goal—to win her back, to take her and Kaley home—and he wasn't about to start a fight that could push her further away. So, he let her go.

"I'll stay here with Grandma," he said smoothly. "You go ahead."

Something was unsettling about his calmness, but Yolaine didn't linger on it. She gathered their things, took Kaley by the hand, and left with Glen.

Janice had been expecting them. She had known for some time that things between Yolaine and Pierce were fractured, and she understood Yolaine's need to get away. The evening passed pleasantly—Martin, Janice's husband, was a gracious host, and their daughter, Caro, was delighted to have company.

Laughter filled the house, games were played, and dinner was lively. But beneath the warmth of the gathering, Janice remained observant.

She watched Glen. She watched Yolaine.

She knew Yolaine well enough to suspect there was more beneath the surface, but tonight, Glen was unreadable. He barely acknowledged Yolaine, keeping himself occupied with Kaley and Caro, avoiding her gaze entirely. He wasn't giving anything away if something was going on between them.

When the night came to a close, Janice made the sleeping arrangements.

"Yolaine, you and Kaley can take the bedroom," she said casually, then turned to Glen. "The guest room's ready for you."

The guest room was small but comfortable.

Glen nodded, offering nothing more.

Whatever had been brewing between him and Yolaine, whatever unspoken storm lingered in the air—it would have to wait.

For now.

That night, Yolaine lay awake in the dark, her body restless, her mind consumed with thoughts of Glen. The house was silent, the only sound the occasional creak of the wooden floorboards as the night settled around her.

Beside her, Kaley slept soundly, her small frame curled beneath the blankets. Yolaine turned onto her side, staring at the ceiling, her heart pounding as temptation gnawed at her.

She had to see him.

She slowly and carefully slipped out of bed, ensuring Kaley remained undisturbed. The house was unfamiliar, and each step was a delicate manoeuvre to avoid making a sound. Janice and Martin's room was at the far end of the hallway, Caro's just next to it.

Glen's room was directly across from hers. His door was slightly ajar—an invitation, a silent understanding between them.

He had anticipated this. He had left it open just for her.

Yolaine pushed the door open just enough to slip inside, shutting it gently behind her and ensuring it remained locked. The faint glow of moonlight filtering through the curtains dimly lit the room.

Glen lay in bed, shirtless, the covers pooled at his waist.

"Glen," she whispered.

He turned towards her, awake, tossing and turning restlessly.

"You came over. I didn't think you'd dare," he murmured, his voice hushed but laced with something deeper—expectation, hunger.

She didn't answer. She moved towards him, the cool air brushing against her bare skin beneath her nightdress.

Glen sat up, reaching for her and pulling her onto his lap. His arms tightened around her waist, drawing her close. His breath was warm against her neck as he pressed a slow kiss below her ear.

"I was hoping you'd come," he murmured, his voice edged with relief. "Happy to see you here."

Yolaine's fingers threaded through Glen's hair, tugging just enough to make him groan as she tipped her head back, giving him access to the delicate column of her throat. His lips moved slowly, teasingly, grazing over her skin, leaving a trail of heat in their wake. His hands roamed over her, slipping beneath her nightgown, his fingers skimming the soft curves of her waist before moving higher, cupping her breasts. A sharp gasp escaped her as his thumbs brushed over her hardened peaks, teasing, kneading, and setting her skin ablaze.

The heat between them grew unbearable. With a swift movement, she pulled her nightgown over her head, letting it fall to the floor in a forgotten heap. The cool air kissed her bare skin, sending a shiver down her spine, but Glen's gaze burned hotter. He took her in—the soft rise and fall of her chest, the way her breasts moved as she shifted in his lap, straddling him completely now.

Their mouths collided, deep and urgent, tongues tangling as he claimed her with a hunger that sent fire rushing through her veins. She rocked against him, feeling the hard evidence of his desire pressing against her through his thin shorts. His grip on her hips tightened, guiding her movements, a low groan vibrating against her lips.

His mouth left hers, trailing lower, teasing the swell of her breasts before capturing a sensitive nipple between his lips. She gasped, her back arching, fingers sinking into his shoulders as he flicked his tongue over her, each touch sending another wave of pleasure surging through her body. His hands wandered lower, squeezing the soft flesh of her thighs, slipping between them, stroking her through the last scrap of fabric she wore.

She needed more—now. In one fluid motion, she lifted her hips and slid her panties down, pushing them off with her legs. The fabric slipped from her ankles, tumbling off the bed, forgotten. Glen's breath hitched as his hands traced her now utterly bare form, his eyes dark with unrestrained desire.

Her fingers slid beneath the waistband of his shorts, wrapping around the thick, rigid heat of him. He groaned, his forehead pressing against her chest, his body shuddering at her touch. She stroked him slowly, deliberately, revelling in the way he twitched against her palm. Then, without breaking eye contact, she helped him push his shorts down, freeing him completely.

Her breath was ragged, her skin flushed as she positioned herself over him, her thighs trembling with anticipation. His hands found her hips, steadying her, guiding her, his fingers pressing into her flesh as she hovered above him.

"Take me," she whispered, her voice thick with need, her lips grazing his ear.

Glen's grip tightened. And as she sank onto him, the world outside ceased to exist. Their bodies moved in a slow, intoxicating rhythm—deliberate, teasing—before surrendering entirely to the wildfire consuming them both.

He didn't start slow. He couldn't. There was no room for restraint, no patience for gentle caresses or whispered confessions. This was raw, desperate—a collision of need and recklessness, stolen in the dead of night beneath another's roof.

His grip on her hips was punishing as he thrust into her, each movement deep, relentless, as if he could brand himself into her skin, claim her in ways that went beyond the physical. Yolaine held on, her arms wound tight around his neck, her forehead pressed against him as their bodies met in a fevered rhythm. Every slam of his hips sent pleasure rocketing through her, tightening the coil inside her belly until she was nothing but sensation.

She wanted to cry out, to let the ecstasy rip through her without restraint, but she couldn't. The walls were too thin, and the risk was too significant. Instead, she bit down on his shoulder, muffling the helpless moan that threatened to escape. Glen hissed at the sting, his breath ragged, his pace growing even more punishing.

"Yolaine," he groaned against her ear. "You feel so good... so tight... taking me so perfectly."

His words ignited something deeper inside her, a primal response she couldn't control. Her body clenched around him, drawing him in even deeper, making him curse under his breath. His hands dug into her waist as he drove into her harder, rougher, pushing her closer to the edge. The bed creaked beneath them, an unforgiving reminder of where they were, of who was just down the hall. But she couldn't care. Not when she was drowning in him, in the heat of his body, in the delicious agony of being stretched and filled over and over again. Her fingers twisted into his hair, tugging, pulling, her body trembling violently as the pleasure mounted to an unbearable peak. The pressure inside her snapped like a taut wire, sending her spiralling into blinding, all-consuming release.

"Glen, I am close..."

"Come for me," Glen urged, his lips brushing her ear, his voice thick with need. And she did. The release crashed over her, blinding, consuming, pulling her under as she buried her face into his neck to stifle her cries.

He wasn't far behind. With a final, deep, shuddering thrust, he groaned into her neck, his body stiffening as he came hard, spilling into her with a raw, primal intensity. She felt every pulse, every hot surge filling her, stretching the high between them until she was lost in it, tangled in pleasure and the reckless abandon of what they had just done.

They stayed tangled together for a moment, their breaths mingling, their bodies still trembling from the aftershocks. Yolaine pressed a lingering kiss to his temple, her fingers stroking his damp hair. But reality was creeping in, reminding her of where they were.

Reluctantly, she pulled away, reaching for her nightdress. Her panties were nowhere to be seen. Frowning, she glanced around until Glen smirked and held them between his fingers.

"They slipped under the bed," he murmured, twirling the fabric teasingly.

She reached for them, but he pulled back, a playful glint in his eyes.

"Let me keep them for the night," he chuckled, husky.

Yolaine narrowed her eyes, a smirk playing on her lips. "You're impossible," she whispered.

He only grinned, tucking them away as if they were his prize.

Sighing, she turned and slowly pulled her nightdress over her body, the soft fabric gliding against her skin. Glen watched her intently, his gaze dark with lingering hunger, his fists clenching as if restraining the urge to pull her back into his arms.

She felt his eyes trace every curve as she smoothed down the fabric, her body still flushed from their time together. He wanted more. She could see it, feel it in the air between them. But he didn't stop her. He knew she had to go.

"Sleep," she whispered.

He smirked. "Not after that."

She bit back a smile and slipped out of the room, careful to make no sound, as she returned to her bed beside Kaley. She lay there, staring at the ceiling, her body still humming with the aftermath of what had just happened.

She had taken a risk—a dangerous one.

And she knew she would do it again.

Early the following day, after breakfast, they left Janice's house. Both thanked her before setting off for home. Just as they were going, Janice called out to Yolaine, her voice gentle yet firm.

"Be careful," she said. "And try to clear the air with Pierce."

Yolaine heard her but didn't react. Did Janice see her sneaking into Glen's room? Had they been watching? The thought flickered through her mind, but she brushed it aside. It didn't matter now. All that mattered was making Glen feel good, reassuring him that she was with him—that he didn't have to worry about everything happening around them.

When they arrived home, Pierce was waiting. His expression was unreadable as he looked at her.

"We're leaving in a short while," he said evenly. "You can always come back to visit Grandma and your parents when they return from their trip."

Yolaine's heart sank. She had known this moment was coming, but hearing it still felt like a blow. She couldn't prolong things any further—it would only put Glen in danger. They packed up in silence. Before leaving, Yolaine pulled Glen aside, her fingers gripping his tighter than usual.

"Take care of yourself," she murmured, searching his eyes. "You're the best person I've ever known—as a friend, partner in crime... and my lovely cousin."

Her words were layered with meaning, with unspoken promises and unfulfilled desires. She wanted him to know that this wasn't goodbye—not really. Glen held her gaze, his jaw tightening slightly, but he nodded. He understood. He always did.

"I will," he said quietly. "And you—stay in touch."

She gave him a small smile, her chest tight, then turned away before the moment's weight could crush her.

Glen stood by the doorway, watching as she climbed into the car and the vehicle pulled away. He didn't wave until the last second, a silent farewell hanging between them.

Then, as the dust settled, he turned and walked back inside the house, where Grandma was waiting. And just like that, she was gone.

# #5
# Restless for You

Yolaine had promised to message Glen when she got home with Pierce and Kaley. The second she stepped through the door, she grabbed her phone and typed, *Just reached home, babes.*

Later that night, unable to resist, she sent another message.

*"I miss you already."*

A string of kisses and hearts followed.

Glen's reply came almost instantly. A slow smile tugged at his lips as his heart kicked up a beat. She hadn't just left him stranded in the afterglow of their stolen moments.

*"All good there?"* he asked.

*"Yes :)"* she replied.

A pause. Then—

*"Are you decent?"*

She grinned at his teasing. *"Yes, I am decent. Don't worry, I won't open up for anyone else except you ;)"* He sent a flood of hearts and smiley faces before dropping something unexpected.

*"I have something of yours."*

Her pulse quickened. *"Oh? What?"*

*"Your panties."*

She inhaled sharply.

*"Soaked in your body's sweat. Smelling like you."*

A shiver ran through her. Her grip tightened around her phone, her lips parting as a familiar heat pooled in her stomach.

*"You're wicked,"* she typed, her fingers trembling slightly.

*"I'll find a way to meet up with you again. Just have patience,"* Yolaine promised.

Glen responded with a big red heart.

*"Let these few days pass. I'll come up with a plan,"* she added, wanting to reassure him— to make sure he didn't feel like she had just left him behind after their time together. She wanted him to know she wasn't only in this for the fun.

A moment passed before his reply came.

*"I'll be waiting."*

They wished each other good night, and with thoughts of each other lingering in their minds, they drifted off to sleep.

The following day, she woke to a voice note from him.

*"Good morning, gorgeous. I dreamt about you. About how you taste, how you feel…"*

His voice was thick with desire, making her thighs clench together. She bit her lip, responding with something just as sultry, sending a picture of her lips slightly parted, her fingers grazing her collarbone suggestively. The game between them had only just begun.

During the day, Yolaine buried herself in work at her brother Edward's fashion design firm. But no matter how much she tried to concentrate, her mind wandered back to Glen. She texted him between tasks, on breaks, and when she stepped through her front door. Every night, just before sleep claimed her, she sent him a message—an indulgence that had quickly become routine.

Glen had returned to his hometown, yet the distance did nothing to quell the fire between them.

At night, their conversations grew wicked. His voice, low and sultry, spilt sinful words into her ear. He guided her through her pleasure while he touched himself on the other end, their desire stretching across the miles.

And so it continued.

"Send me a video," he murmured one evening, his voice thick with want.

She hesitated, her pulse quickening. "What do you want to see?"

"All of you."

"You already have—in every way imaginable," she replied with a teasing smile emoji.

"I want to refresh my memory," he shot back smoothly.

A slow smirk curved her lips as she set up her phone. She slid the straps of her nightdress from her shoulders, letting them fall to her waist. Her fingers glided over her bare skin, a deliberate tease, knowing he was watching.

"Goodness, Yolaine... you've no idea what you do to me," he groaned.

She laughed softly, revelling in the effect she had on him. "Then show me."

And he did.

A video followed—a slow, torturous stroke, his breath ragged, his body tight with restraint until he finally gave in, moaning her name. She watched, captivated, as heat curled deep inside her.

With Pierce starting his business trips, as usual, Yolaine often had the house to herself. The solitude only intensified her cravings for Glen.

One night, unable to resist any longer, she video-called him, her body already aching for his touch.

She let her nightdress slip from her shoulders as soon as he answered, baring herself entirely to him.

"*I need you,*" she whispered, spreading her legs on the bed, her fingers trailing down her stomach, lower, teasing herself as he watched.

Glen groaned. "*Babbeeeey, touch yourself for me. Let me see you.*"

She grabbed a pillow, pressing it between her thighs, grinding against it, her breath catching as the friction sent jolts of pleasure through her body.

"*Like this?*" she teased, rolling her hips.

"*Just like that,*" Glen rasped. "*Ride it for me. I want to see you move.*"

She adjusted the phone camera, giving him a perfect view as she rocked against the pillow, her moans soft and needy. Her fingers toyed with her nipples, sending electric sparks through her body.

"*You're so beautiful,*" he panted. "*I wish I were there, spreading you open, f..king you properly.*"

Her body tensed as waves of pleasure crashed over her, her moans muffled into the pillow. Glen followed right after, his release spilling over his hand, his breath ragged.

But he wasn't done.

"*Turn around,*" he ordered, his voice thick with desire. "*Get on your hands and knees for me.*"

A shiver ran down Yolaine's spine. She obeyed, arching her back, wriggling her hips, teasing him.

"*Is this what you wanted?*" she whispered. "*I'm bending for you... can you drive me through?*"

Glen let out a sharp breath, his grip tightening on the phone. "*You're going to be the death of me.*"

She smirked. "*For now, I want to see you stroke yourself for me.*"

"*Only if you keep bending for me,*" he countered.

"*Sure, darling. Anything for you.*"

Glen leaned back, his hand wrapping around his thick, aching length. He stroked himself, his breath ragged, his eyes fixed on her. The pleasure built until he groaned, releasing in hot, shuddering waves.

Yolaine watched, mesmerised by the sight of his release spilling over his hand. A wicked smile curved her lips.

*"Next time I see you, I'll swallow every drop and clean you dry."*

Glen groaned at her words, his body still trembling from his climax. *"I can't wait now."*

Yolaine giggled, glancing over her shoulder, knowing exactly how much power she held over him.

*"I don't mind if you suffer a little,"* she teased. *"As long as you enjoy it."*

*"You're evil,"* Glen muttered. *"And I love it."*

They continued like this for days—naughty texts, teasing pictures, naughty video calls. Yolaine felt alive again. She had found something intoxicating with Glen, something wild and unrestrained.

She didn't care what Pierce thought. She didn't care what the world expected. For now, she was happy. And nothing else mattered.

Pierce was back from his business trip. It didn't take him long to notice Yolaine's changed behaviour—she was almost always on her phone after work or just before drifting off to sleep. But he didn't say a word. He couldn't. He wasn't in any position to question her, to check on her, or to comment. Not anymore. Instead, he focused on being a supportive husband and an attentive father. He spent most of his time with Kaley whenever he could, throwing himself into the role as if it could somehow make up for everything he'd broken.

Pierce knew the truth—Yolaine had caught him red-handed, undeniable evidence of his infidelity laid bare. And though she had every reason to leave, she chose to stay—for the kids' sake, and maybe for her reasons, though he wasn't naive enough to think love was one of them anymore. The marriage hung together by fraying threads, more of an understanding than a true partnership. After putting Kaley to bed one weekend night, Yolaine slipped beneath the covers with a quiet sigh. Pierce was already lying beside her, scrolling absently through his phone, the pale light casting soft reflections across his face. They hadn't spoken much that evening—just the usual polite exchanges about dinner and Kaley's bedtime routine. The silence between them had become familiar, almost comfortable in its distance.

"One of my relatives is getting married," Yolaine said flatly. "I'll attend the wedding and stay at their house."

It was in another town, a few hours' drive away. Pierce glanced up from his phone, sensing an opportunity.

"I'll come with you," he offered, sitting up slightly as though eager to close the gap between them. Yolaine froze for a moment. She hadn't wanted him to come along. She knew all too well how easily he could charm her family—how her parents still looked at him as if he were the perfect son-in-law. A smooth talker, always wearing the right mask.

But she said nothing. It would do Kaley some good to have her father there. Pierce was often absent, either swallowed up by business trips or glued to his phone.

"Fine," she replied after a long pause, her tone unreadable.

And just like that, it was settled. Even if the air between them remained thick with things left unsaid.

Yolaine turned onto her side of the bed, the glow from her phone illuminating her face. Across from her, Pierce continued scrolling aimlessly through his screen, the quiet between them as vast as ever—almost soothing in its emptiness.

Her fingers danced over the keyboard as she messaged Glen.

Yolaine: *Rosie's getting married. I'll go to the wedding and stay for a few days.* His reply came almost instantly.

Glen: *That's nice. You need a bit of a break. Family time will do you good, love.* A faint smile tugged at her lips. She hesitated, then typed again.

Yolaine: *Will you be there?*

There was a short pause before his response came through.

Glen: *I don't think so. Mum and Dad will be going, though.*

He was referring to his parents—her aunt and uncle. Yolaine stared at his message for a moment. It surprised her; Glen rarely missed family gatherings. But she understood. With Pierce tagging along, having Glen there would only complicate things.

Yolaine: *It's a shame you're not coming. I'll miss seeing you.*

Glen: *I'll miss you too. But if I were there, I wouldn't get a chance to have you all to myself... and you know how greedy I am when it comes to you.*

She bit her lip, feeling the familiar flutter deep in her belly.

Yolaine: *You always know what to say...*

Glen: *Because I know what you like. What you need.*

Yolaine: *And what's that, Glen?*

Glen: *Me. Whispering in your ear and touching you the way no one else can.*

Her breath caught as she read his words.

Yolaine: *You drive me mad.*

Glen: *Good. I want you restless. Thinking about me when you're lying next to him.*

Yolaine: *I do... every night.* There was a pause, and then his following message appeared.

Glen: *You should get some rest now. Dream of me tonight.*

Yolaine: *Always. Goodnight, darling.*

Glen: *Goodnight, my beautiful girl. Kisses... everywhere.*

She smiled softly as she set her phone down on the nightstand. The longing didn't ease, but it was enough to carry her into sleep.

Yolaine stopped by her brother Edward's office the next day at work. She leaned casually against the doorframe before stepping inside.

"I need to take a day off," she said, watching him glance up from his sketches. "Rosie's wedding is this weekend. We don't work weekends, but I might need Monday off, depending on how things go."

Edward smiled warmly, setting his pencil aside. "Of course," he said. "You should be there. Someone from the family has to go since I can't make it."

He sighed, shaking his head. "Far too much going on here. But I'm glad you can represent us."

Family meant everything to them. They'd always tried to show up for one another—whether for weddings, celebrations, or when standing together through difficult times. It kept their bond strong, even as life constantly pulled them in different directions.

Later that afternoon, during her break, Yolaine messaged Glen again.

Yolaine: *Are you sure you can't come? I'm travelling there.... It would be good to see you, too.*

She hesitated, then added:

Yolaine: *Pierce will be there, though.*

Several minutes passed in silence before his reply came through.

Glen: *Yeah,... best I sit this one out. I wouldn't want things to get awkward.*

She understood. It wasn't enjoyable, but she wasn't going to push him. They both knew it wasn't simple anymore.

After that, they left the topic alone and drifted into other conversations—light-hearted messages that helped them focus on their day. Yolaine returned to her work at Edward's firm while Glen buried himself in his university assignments. Yet beneath the casual words and ordinary tasks, the pull between them remained constant and undeniable.

… #6

# Where There's Will, There's a Way

Yolaine, Pierce, and Kaley arrived at Rosie's house on Friday evening, just two days before the wedding. The entire family was already there, including Glen's mum, dad, and younger sister. The house buzzed with warmth and laughter, and everyone gathered in cheerful conversation. It was the kind of scene that should have felt comforting and familiar.

Kaley wasted no time getting swept up with her cousins, running off hand-in-hand with them, her delighted squeals filling the house. Yolaine watched her daughter with a soft smile. At least Kaley was happy.

Rosie's house was big enough to accommodate most of the relatives, though a few had chosen to stay in serviced apartments nearby. Yolaine managed to secure a bedroom inside the house for herself, Pierce, and Kaley. It wasn't exactly what she wanted, but it made sense—practical and appropriate.

As the evening wore on, Yolaine found herself missing Glen. She knew he wasn't coming—or at least, he'd said he wasn't. Still, the ache of his absence lingered. After Kaley had gone to bed and Pierce was once again lost in his phone, Yolaine slipped under the covers and messaged Glen.

Their night conversation was the usual mix of light teasing and quiet longing.

Yolaine: *I wish you were here...*

Glen: *You know why I'm not. It wouldn't be easy.*

Yolaine: *Still... I'd like to see you.*

Glen: *You'll dream of me anyway.*

She smiled faintly at his words, wishing she could have more than messages and imagination. After a while, they said goodnight, and Yolaine settled into sleep with her phone tucked close on the nightstand.

The following day was a whirlwind. Everyone was busy helping out—organising the decorations, finalising the arrangements at the venue, and handling the endless stream of details that weddings demanded. Yolaine threw herself into the work, partly to stay distracted, partly because it was expected of her.

And then, sometime in the afternoon, Glen walked in.

He strolled through the doorway as if he'd always planned to be there, a duffel bag slung over his shoulder and that familiar, easy smile on his face. The room seemed to brighten. His mum was the first to spot him, her face lighting up with surprise and delight. Soon, everyone buzzed around him, welcoming him back into the fold with hugs and cheerful teasing about his last-minute arrival.

Yolaine's heart thudded. She kept her expression neutral, smiling like everyone else, but inside, she struggled to stay composed. She greeted him politely when it was her turn—just another cousin in a crowd of family—but there was a flicker in Glen's eyes when they met hers, something that said he felt it too.

The rest of the day was excruciating. They were careful, keeping their distance when others were around, but every stolen glance burned with what they couldn't say aloud. When they finally got a brief moment alone in the kitchen—amid the bustle of preparing tea and setting out biscuits—Yolaine couldn't help herself.

"What made you change your mind?" she asked quietly, keeping her back to him as she poured hot water into mugs. "I wasn't expecting you."

Glen stepped closer, close enough that she could feel his warmth without him even touching her. "I couldn't stay away," he said softly. "I told myself it was complicated, that it was better if I didn't come... but then I thought about you being here. I couldn't resist."

Yolaine glanced at him over her shoulder, a faint grin tugging at her lips.

"I'm glad you came," she said in a low voice. "Even if it's awkward."

"Awkward's a small price to pay," Glen murmured. His hand brushed hers briefly as he took one of the mugs. It was nothing anyone would notice. But it was enough to make her pulse race.

For the rest of the day, they settled into the rhythm of family duties, slipping in the occasional text message whenever they could steal a moment of privacy.

That night, Glen slept in the living room with the other cousins. They'd set up a makeshift camp on the floor—blankets, pillows, and sleeping bags strewn everywhere. He'd laughed along with the others, telling stories and joining in the late-night games, but occasionally, he caught Yolaine watching him from across the room.

And later, after Kaley was asleep and Pierce lay turned away from her, the phone still glowing faintly in his hand, Yolaine lay beneath the covers and messaged Glen one last time.

Yolaine: *I can't believe you're here... and I still have to pretend I don't miss you.*

Glen: *I'm here. Close enough that if you close your eyes, you'll feel me.*

She sighed, a quiet, restless sound in the dark.

Yolaine: *Goodnight, Glen.*

Glen: *Goodnight, my beautiful girl. Dream of me...*

Early the next morning—the wedding event day—the house was already alive with activity. It buzzed like a lively marketplace: people dashing in and out of rooms, voices raised over one another, laughter mixed with instructions, and the constant thud of hurried footsteps across the floors. Rosie's mother was everywhere, giving orders and trying her best to keep things from chaos.

In the middle of it all, she approached Yolaine. "Could you pop over to the venue and check the banquet hall and the bride and groom's suites? Make sure everything's in order before we head there," she said, flustered but relieved to have someone dependable to ask.

It was the perfect break Yolaine had been hoping for. It was utterly unexpected... and she wasn't going to waste it. "Of course, Auntie," she replied, keeping her tone steady and helpful, concealing the excitement already building.

The resort where the wedding was to be held was only a few miles away. Without hesitating, Yolaine slipped away and rang Glen.

*"Come with me,"* she said softly but firmly. *"We'll check the venue together."*

A short while later, Glen met her outside. He was casually dressed, his usual easy smirk tugging at the corner of his mouth. They were about to get into the car when Yolaine caught sight of Pierce standing by the door. Arms folded across his chest; he was watching them. Kaley was inside somewhere with her cousins, but Pierce's eyes never left Yolaine.

"I'm heading to the venue," she said lightly as if it was unimportant. "With Glen. Keep an eye on Kaley for me."

Pierce didn't reply immediately. His gaze flickered to Glen, then back to her. A man like Pierce noticed everything. But for now, he kept his thoughts to himself. After a moment, he nodded. "Take Glen's mum along," he said coolly. "You'll need all the help you can get."

Yolaine smiled, tight and controlled. "Good idea." Standing nearby, she approached Glen's mother and invited her to join them.

Moments later, they were all in the car—Yolaine driving, Glen beside her in the front seat, his mother sitting quietly in the back.

Yolaine's mind raced as they drove, but she was calm outwardly. Now and then, Glen's leg brushed against hers, a subtle jolt each time, but he remained composed, conversing politely with his mother as they passed by fields and winding roads.

Soon, they arrived at the resort. Staff were already bustling about, putting the final touches on the preparations. Yolaine put on her responsible face, efficiently meeting with the event coordinator, reviewing the checklist, and walking through the arrangements—seating plans, floral decorations, lighting, and catering details. Glen and his mother accompanied her, ticking boxes and asking questions.

But underneath it all, Yolaine's mind was elsewhere. And Glen knew it.

After an hour or so, Yolaine turned to Glen's mother. "Auntie, would you mind reviewing the seating arrangements one last time? And perhaps have a word with the caterers about the timings?" she suggested, her voice casual but persuasive. "I'll check the bride and groom's suites."

Glen's mother nodded at once. "Of course, love," she said. "I'll make sure it's all sorted."

As soon as she was gone, Yolaine glanced at Glen. His brow quirked in quiet amusement; he already knew what was coming. They walked side by side toward the bridal suites, their pace unhurried until they reached the door. Yolaine slipped her hand into her pocket, retrieved the key, and opened it. They stepped inside, closing the door softly behind them.

The faint click of the lock echoed in the hush, and before the sound had faded, Yolaine turned. She caught Glen by the front of his shirt and pulled him towards her. Their mouths met in a fierce, hungry kiss, breath mingling as they stumbled backwards, laughter catching in their throats.

Glen steadied them both, one arm tight around her waist, the other flicking the lock into place without looking. He barely got the chance to breathe before Yolaine was tugging at his clothes, fingers impatient and eager.

"I've been wanting this for days," she whispered, her voice low and thick with longing.

"So have I," he murmured against the curve of her neck, his lips brushing her skin as his hands slipped beneath the hem of her loose top. "I knew what you were up to the moment you called."

She gave a wicked little smile. "And you came running anyway."

The bridal suite was silent, an oasis of calm away from the chaos beyond its walls. But here, the air was charged, thick with anticipation. Glen's gaze caught hers, dark and smouldering, and without another word, he reached for her. His fingers laced through hers, tugging her closer until their bodies met, chest to chest, hips pressed tight.

His kiss this time was slow, deliberate. A claiming. His lips were warm, his tongue teasing, making her shiver as need coiled hot and fast inside her. Her hands slid up to cup his jaw, then wound around his neck, pulling him deeper into the kiss.

She could feel the thump of his heartbeat against her own; their bodies were already wound tight with desire. Glen's hands traced a slow path down, slipping beneath her top. His palms were warm against her skin as he lifted the loose fabric over her head, drawing it away and tossing it aside.

His gaze dropped to her bra, and a low sound rumbled in his throat. "You're exquisite," he breathed.

Yolaine arched towards him in answer, offering herself without shame. Glen didn't hesitate. His fingers pushed under the cups of her bra, lifting them to bare her breasts to his hungry gaze. He dipped his head and took one nipple between his lips, his tongue flicking in slow, decadent circles. Yolaine gasped, her fingers sinking into his hair, holding him closer.

"Glen..." she sighed, breath catching.

He suckled at her with the reverence of a man worshipping something sacred, taking his time, lavishing attention until she was trembling beneath his mouth. Her hand slid down the line of his body, finding the button of his jeans and popping it open. The zip followed, and her fingers slipped inside to wrap around the heat and hardness she found waiting for her. He was already hard, thick and pulsing in her palm.

A groan rumbled deep in his chest, vibrating against her skin. He pulled back, their eyes locking as he whispered, "Not on the bed. It's meant for them."

Yolaine's lips curved into a slow, wicked grin. "Then take me somewhere else."

He didn't need to tell twice. Glen guided her backwards, his hands roaming over her body as he steered her toward the couch next to the bed. He laid her down gently, his touch reverent, though his eyes blazed with urgency.

Quickly, he kicked off his jeans and reached for her. She lifted her hips, helping him peel off her tight jeans and panties in one go. As soon as they were gone, Yolaine opened her legs unabashed, her gaze locked on his.

Glen groaned at the sight of her, lowering himself between her thighs. His mouth found her heat, kissing her softly at first, then with growing hunger. His tongue explored her, slow strokes that made her moan, her fingers weaving through his hair as she held him close.

But soon, it wasn't enough. She needed more.

"Glen," she breathed, trembling, "I need you. Now."

He rose, lips glistening, and without a word, positioned himself at her entrance. With a slow, deep thrust, he filled her, pushing inside until he was buried to the hilt. Yolaine bit her lip to stifle the cry that tore from her throat, her fingers digging into his shoulders as she adjusted to his size.

"I missed you," Glen murmured against her ear, his voice rough.

"Stop talking," she whispered, desire thick in her tone. "Just have me."

He chuckled, a low, wicked sound, and then he moved. His hips rocked against hers in a rhythm that was at first deliberate, teasing but quickly built into something more urgent. Her legs wrapped around his waist, urging him deeper, harder.

Glen leaned down, taking one of her nipples into his mouth again as he thrust into her, his tongue flicking over the sensitive peak while his hips drove harder. Yolaine gasped, her back arching, meeting him stroke for stroke.

"Faster," she urged, breathless. "We don't have much time."

"I can't help it," he groaned. "I need you more."

Her body answered him, hips lifting to meet his thrusts, slick and desperate. She could feel him stretching her folds, pushing deep, the friction sending sparks through her. Her hands slid down to grip his bottoms, pulling him closer, more profound.

"Come for me," she whispered against his mouth, their kiss messy and urgent. "I'm so close…"

His rhythm faltered just slightly as his body tensed. "I'm coming," he growled.

"Don't stop," she gasped. "I'm coming too…"

Their cries blended as they crashed over the edge together. Yolaine quivered beneath him, her body tightening around Glen as his release surged through her. He jerked a little more, spilling inside her with one last, deep thrust. They collapsed there, a breathless tangle of limbs, skin slick with sweat and the glow of fulfilled desire, hearts pounding in sync as they caught their breath.

The quiet after was almost tender. Glen kissed her damp forehead before easing back, his breathing still ragged. Yolaine smiled lazily, stretching out beneath him before sitting up.

"We've got to get a move on," Yolaine said, her voice carrying a cheeky little tease. She slid up to grab her dress, but Glen tugged her back into his arms, wrapping her in a tight hug. "Glen, we need to scarper," she urged, though a smile tugged at her lips. He didn't say a word—just pressed a soft kiss to her shoulder, holding her close, his fingers tickling her sides. Yolaine squirmed, loving it, but well aware they'd be missed if they didn't shift soon.

He let out a quiet chuckle, easing her to her feet. They scrambled into their clothes, fumbling with buttons and zips, smoothing wild hair, and brushing at flushed cheeks. Yolaine darted to the mirror, tweaking her loose top into place, while Glen raked a hand through his hair, shaking his head with a lopsided grin.

"You're trouble," he murmured, voice low and warm, as they made for the door.

"And you love it," she replied with a wink.

One last glance to ensure the room was just as they found it, and then they slipped out, heading back to Glen's mother's waiting. Their secret burned bright between them, hidden—for now.

The drive home was quiet, save for the low hum of the engine and the faint strains of music playing from the car stereo. Yolaine's hands rested lightly on the steering wheel; fingers relaxed yet deliberate as she navigated the familiar winding roads. The late afternoon sun hung low, casting its golden warmth across the landscape, making the fields shimmer as if dusted in light.

Beside her, Glen sat in easy silence, his arm resting loosely on the door. His gaze was turned outward, but Yolaine could feel his quiet attention—a presence that seemed to hum in the confined space between them. In the back seat, Glen's mother hummed softly to herself, her hands folded neatly in her lap, the tune almost matching the rhythm of the car's steady movement.

There was calm now. The earlier intensity—the secret, burning moments shared in the bridal suite—had softened into something quiet and potent—unspoken but there.

As they pulled up in front of the house, Yolaine shifted the gear into the park and turned the key, the engine fading into silence. Glen was the first to move, his motions unhurried, yet there was a glint in his eyes that hadn't been there before—that unmistakable glint of satisfaction. His gaze met hers briefly before he stepped out, his lips curving faintly, knowingly.

Glen's mother followed, smoothing the front of her dress as she climbed out. She gave Yolaine a gentle smile before adjusting her shawl.

Pierce was already there, waiting at the front door. He leaned casually against the doorframe, arms folded across his chest in a stance that could almost seem relaxed. But Yolaine knew him better. His gaze flicked toward them, lingering on her longer than necessary before he offered a faint smile. It didn't quite reach his eyes.

She stepped out, her movements graceful as always, smoothing herself as she walked toward Kaley. Pierce's eyes followed her, but he didn't say anything. Glen remained near his mother, and they walked into the house.

Down in the grass, Kaley crouched, wholly absorbed in her dolls and their tiny tea set. Her curls bounced as she moved, her little hands carefully arranging the cups as though the world beyond her game didn't exist.

"I fed her," Pierce said, his voice even. Measured. "She was hungry."

Yolaine gave a slight nod as she unfastened her seatbelt. "Thank you," she said quietly.

Yolaine crouched beside her daughter. "What did you have, sweetheart?" she asked, her voice soft, maternal.

Kaley didn't glance up. "Daddy fed me food."

"That's good," Yolaine murmured, brushing a loose curl from Kaley's forehead. "Was it yummy?"

"Mmmhmm," Kaley replied absently, still deep in her game. "It was yummy, Mama."

Yolaine smiled faintly, leaning in to kiss Kaley's temple before rising smoothly to her feet. Without another glance toward Pierce, she walked toward the house, her steps unhurried but sure. She could still feel Pierce's eyes on her back as she disappeared inside.

Inside the quiet sanctuary of her bedroom, Yolaine closed the door behind her with a soft click. She stood there for a long moment, leaning against it, breathing deeply. The house muffled everything—the footsteps, the voices. She was alone.

She crossed to her vanity with deliberate grace. Slowly, methodically, she freshened up. She undressed, slipping out of her soaked panties with a faint shiver at the dampness. She stepped into a fresh pair, smoothing them over her hips. But she felt it again within moments—wetness pooling, soaking the fabric. She washed her face, cool water banishing the flush of the afternoon. She reapplied a hint of makeup—just enough to restore her calm mask—and brushed her hair until it shone, dark and smooth. Her fingers lingered on the simple gold chain around her neck, adjusting it until it rested perfectly at her throat.

Her reflection watched her with calm eyes. No judgment. No shame. Just knowing.

When she returned to the living room, the mood had changed. Warmth had replaced the earlier chill. Glen was laughing softly at something his mother said, and Pierce was seated at the far end of the sofa, sipping from a glass of water, his body language more relaxed. Kaley had wandered inside, too, sitting cross-legged on the carpet with her dolls lined up in perfect rows.

The family gathered, talking quickly. Even Pierce thawed a little, sharing the occasional remark that drew laughter from the group.

Glen's phone buzzed quietly in his palm. He glanced at the screen, lips twitching into a grin.

Are you okay? Yolaine's message glowed softly.

He typed back:

I am. You?

Her reply came swiftly.

Still wet.

His fingers paused. A slow grin spread across his face.

Then don't wear panties, he typed.

Her answer:

I put on a fresh pair. They're soaked now, too.

His pulse spiked.

Take them off, he wrote.

Her next reply was swift, teasing.

Are you mad? My dress will get wet. They'll all see.

The game continued, their conversation threading through the rest of the evening like a dangerous secret. Between sips of tea, between idle comments to their families, their messages pulsed in their hands like a second, private language.

As the sun dipped lower and evening descended, the house came alive with quiet excitement. Rosie's wedding celebration was drawing near.

Yolaine dressed Kaley, brushing her curls and tying them back with a soft pink ribbon. Kaley's gown was delicate, blush pink with layers of tulle that made her look like a storybook princess. Yolaine fastened her shoes with gentle fingers, then lifted her daughter into her arms.

"You look like a princess," she whispered, kissing Kaley's cheek.

Kaley giggled, throwing her arms around her mother's neck in a warm hug. Yolaine held her close, breathing her in.

Rosie was ready when Yolaine and the others joined her in the hallway.

She was radiant, and her gown elegant—understated yet undeniably stunning. With each movement, the silk caught the light, a quiet shimmer that made her appear almost ethereal. Her bouquet of blush roses and white peonies rested delicately in her hands, the soft colours complementing her natural grace.

They left for the venue together, the small procession slipping into their respective cars. Yolaine sat beside Rosie's mother in the bridal car, its bonnet adorned with fresh flowers and satin ribbons, while Glen and the cousins drove ahead in a convoy of sleek vehicles. Pierce followed in his car, Kaley safely nestled in the back seat, her pink tulle dress puffed up around her like a cloud.

At the venue—a grand manor house set amidst sweeping gardens—Rosie's groom, Michael, waited for her at the entrance. He stood just beneath the portico, adjusting his cufflinks with fingers that trembled slightly. The moment Rosie stepped out of the car, his entire face softened. His nervous tension melted into something gentler, his eyes holding nothing but adoration. Rosie crossed to him without hesitation, slipping her hand into his as though they had always belonged that way.

Together, they entered the bridal room, accompanied by their closest family members—Yolaine and Pierce—offering quiet encouragement and last-minute adjustments. Yolaine's hands were steady as she smoothed Rosie's veil into place, her fingers careful not to disturb the delicate beading. Pierce gave Michael's tie one final, precise adjustment, clasping his shoulder with a brief nod of approval.

As Yolaine stepped back, her gaze drifted around the room. The air was fragrant with roses, the soft glow of candles casting a gentle light over everything. But it wasn't the beauty of the setting that held her attention—it was the memory that stirred in her chest. She had been here earlier. With Glen. In this very room. Their bodies tangled in breathless abandon, his scent lingering faintly in the air, the ghost of his touch sparking against her skin. She closed her eyes for a brief moment, feeling it again—the way his hands had mapped her curves, the heat of his mouth at her throat—a secret they both carried in silence.

Tradition dictated that the groom should not see his bride before the ceremony. It was said to be bad luck. But Michael and Rosie had never put much stock in old superstitions. They wanted to be together, even in these final moments before they stood before their guests. And so, they stood side by side now, whispering to one another, fingers laced, utterly unconcerned by what others might think.

It was their day, and they would live it their way.

Once all the guests arrived, they were told to join in.

The ceremony was held beneath an arch of roses and wisteria in the garden, and fairy lights were strung above them like a canopy of stars. Rosie walked down the aisle on her father's arm, her smile luminous. Michael's eyes never left her. The vows were exchanged beneath the soft murmur of doves in the trees. Rings slipped onto trembling fingers. A kiss sealed their promises, drawing warm applause from the guests.

The celebration that followed was a vision from a dream. As dusk fell, lanterns glowed softly, illuminating the dance floor. The first dance belonged to Rosie and Michael, their movements graceful as the music swelled—an elegant waltz played by the string quartet.

Afterwards, the floor filled with couples. Yolaine danced with Pierce, their daughter between them, giggling as they turned. Glen danced nearby, but his gaze strayed too often. Whenever they passed one another, Yolaine and Glen exchanged private glances thick with meaning. They kept their distance, but it was careful, deliberate, and temporary.

Dinner was a lavish affair in the grand dining hall. Exquisite courses were served on fine china: roasted lamb with rosemary, seabass in delicate blanc, and towers of fresh fruits and cheeses. Vintage wines poured freely, and laughter and the clink of glasses rang through the hall. The desserts were artful—miniature pastries, glistening tarts, and a towering wedding cake of vanilla sponge and sugared flowers.

Speeches followed, heartfelt and joyous. Toasts were raised again and again. Rosie and Michael beamed at one another, holding hands beneath the table, eyes only for each other.

At last, the couple departed beneath a shower of rose petals, their car driving off into the night, tin cans clattering behind.

Later, as the hall emptied and candles guttered low, Yolaine found Glen standing quietly with his cousins. She approached, her steps slow, deliberate.

"You're looking very handsome in your suit," she murmured as she passed him.

He turned, catching her gaze. "And you," he said softly, "look like the princess of my dreams."

Yolaine's lips curved into a faint smile. She leaned closer, her breath warm against his ear. "Do you know something?"

"What?" Glen asked, voice husky.

"I'm not wearing any panties underneath," she whispered.

His pulse thundered in his ears. He stared at her, unable to move, heart in his throat.

Yolaine stepped away, glancing back at him once, eyes dark with promise, before walking toward Pierce, who was waiting for her. They climbed into their car, Pierce's hand steady on her back as he opened the door.

Glen stood frozen, watching, helpless to act. He could do nothing but watch Yolaine walk away. After a moment, he joined his cousins in their car. The road home stretched ahead, but Glen's mind was already elsewhere—trapped in the heat of Yolaine's whispered confession and her hips' slow, deliberate sway as she disappeared from view.

#7

# The Silent Connection

Glen and his cousins decided to stop by Tat's Ice Cream Parlour on their way home. They were in no rush, and the night still felt young. They ordered a round of ice cream—double scoops all around—and settled into a corner booth, laughing, joking, and catching up like old times. For a little while, everything felt easy and light.

Meanwhile, Yolaine, Pierce, Kaley and the rest of the family reached home. The house gradually quietened as everyone settled down for the night. But Yolaine noticed something. Glen and the others weren't back yet.

She picked up her phone and rang him.

"Miss me already?" Glen answered his tone teasing, followed by a soft laugh.

"Very funny," Yolaine said, rolling her eyes. "Where are you all?"

"We're at Tat's, having ice cream," Glen replied casually.

Yolaine huffed. "Not fair! Why didn't you tell us? We would've joined."

"You still can," Glen said. "Come over."

Yolaine smiled faintly but shook her head. "Kaley's already drowsy. I need to settle her down. You lot go ahead."

By the time Glen and his cousins finally returned, it was late. The house was dark, and everyone was already asleep. They tiptoed inside, careful not to wake anyone, and found their way to the makeshift beds in the living room. One by one, they settled down for the night.

Just as Glen was about to close his eyes, his phone buzzed softly.

Are you back? It was Yolaine.

He stared at the screen momentarily, then put the phone aside without answering. He lay down, pulling the blanket over himself, exhaling slowly.

Another buzz. This time, just a simple:?

Glen sighed and picked up the phone. Yes, I'm back. In the living room, he typed back. He hesitated momentarily, staring at the glowing screen, wondering if there would be another message.

Yolaine responded *I miss you, you duffer...*

Glen replied, *You're a big duffer—telling me you weren't wearing panties and then walking away like that...*

Yolaine grinned at her screen. *Only for you, sweetheart.*

Glen's fingers flew over the keys. *I didn't even get to admire you properly, so what was the point?*

Yolaine shot back. You *can have it now if you want.*

*Now? Are you crazy?* Glen typed.

*The best things come unexpectedly,* Yolaine replied smoothly.

*You're mad,* Glen sent back.

*You're sweet,* came Yolaine's reply.

*Yeah, I know that* Glen smirked at his screen.

Then her message appeared: *Meet me on the terrace.*

*Now? Are you serious?* Glen replied.

*Oh, I'm serious,* she answered. *Everyone's dead tired and fast asleep anyway.* Glen's heart thudded as he slowly got up from the makeshift bed. He crept, careful not to wake his cousins. Slipping past them, he went to the staircase leading up to the bedrooms. He passed Yolaine's room on his way to the attic, where a narrow passage took him up to the terrace.

The night sky stretched wide and dark above him, painted silver by the moonlight. Dawn wasn't far off.

He waited.

A few minutes later, his phone buzzed. It was Yolaine: *I can't come over. Pierce is still awake—he's turning about. I'm so sorry...*

Glen replied: *That's fine. Don't take any risks, please.*

He lingered on the terrace a bit longer, alone under the quiet sky, before heading back down and settling into his makeshift bed.

The following day, the house was alive with commotion. Yolaine was busy tending to Kaley; Pierce was occupied with the other elders in the family. Slowly, one by one, the relatives said their goodbyes and left.

Glen and his family were also getting ready to leave. Yolaine, Pierce, and Kaley stood at the door, bidding farewell.

Everyone exchanged hugs and kisses. Except Glen.

He nodded at Yolaine, gave her a casual *bye*, and left with his family.

Yolaine watched him go, a sinking feeling settling in her chest. She realised Glen was upset because of the night before.

Later, she sent him a message: *Are you okay?*

There was no response.

Yolaine, Pierce, and Kaley had a long drive back home. The car hummed steadily along the road, but Yolaine's mind was elsewhere. She knew Glen was upset about what had happened the night before—or rather, what hadn't happened. She shouldn't have promised to meet him and then backed out. It had been reckless, saying yes when she knew the risks. She'd let herself get carried away at the moment, and now the weight of her regret sat heavily on her chest.

She was older and more experienced. She should have handled it better. She should have handled *him* better. Glen was younger, yes, but he was earnest. And last night, she'd hurt him.

Yolaine kept glancing at her phone, willing a message to appear. Nothing. Glen was silent. She was stuck. She couldn't call him—Pierce was right beside her. All she could do was wait and count the minutes until they reached home. The silence stretched endlessly.

Finally, unable to bear it any longer, she typed a message.

*Hey... what's up? Reply, please.*

By the time they finally reached home, it was early evening. The drive had been long and quiet, the atmosphere thick with unspoken thoughts. Yolaine went about settling Kaley, who was already drowsy, into her evening routine. Once Kaley was comfortable and resting, Yolaine retreated to their bedroom. She closed the door behind her with a soft sigh and made her way to the bathroom. She let the water run over her, hoping it might wash away the unease that clung to her skin. After her bath, she stood in front of the mirror, towel-drying herself absent-mindedly. Her gaze flicked towards her phone on the countertop—still nothing from Glen.

She stared at the blank screen for a moment longer before finally picking up the phone and calling him. It rang, but he didn't answer. Her heart sank a little further. Perhaps he needed time. She told herself to be patient and set the phone aside, though it wasn't easy.

Yolaine forced herself to focus on the evening ahead. She got dressed, tied her damp hair up, and joined Pierce downstairs. He was sitting on the sofa, phone in hand, fingers tapping away as he caught up on work emails. They exchanged a few casual words, but their conversations these days lacked warmth. Yolaine busied herself by tidying up and then retreated to her tasks. That night, when she climbed into bed, sleep eluded her. Her mind kept drifting back to Glen—his silence, the ache of his absence, and the guilt gnawing at her for making promises she hadn't kept. She wanted to talk to him. She needed to explain.

But she couldn't force it. The night passed restlessly. She tossed and turned, her thoughts tangled up in Glen's last expression before he left, the quiet goodbye without the usual warmth.

The following day came far too quickly. Yolaine rose early, as always. She helped Kaley get ready for school with the assistance of their maid. Once Kaley was on her way, Yolaine prepared herself for work. There was no choice but to face the day ahead. She had taken leave for the wedding, and now the backlog of work was waiting for her. By mid-morning, she was fully absorbed in tasks—reports, meetings, and emails. It was easier to stay distracted.

But when her workload finally eased in the late afternoon, she found herself staring at her phone again. The empty screen gnawed at her patience.

Taking a breath, she sent him another message.

*Hi... You, okay? Please message me back, sweetheart.*

She set the phone down, telling herself not to expect much. Minutes passed. Then, finally, the screen lit up.

*Hi,* came Glen's reply.

A single word, but it was enough.

Without hesitation, Yolaine called him. He answered on the second ring.

"Hi," Glen said, his voice neutral.

"Duffer! Idiot!" Yolaine scolded, though there was relief in her tone. "Why didn't you take my call? Why didn't you reply to my messages?"

There was a pause before Glen answered quietly, "I felt... like I was getting in between you and Pierce. Like I shouldn't forget you've got your own life."

Yolaine's heart clenched. "I have nothing with Pierce," she said firmly. "I only didn't want to take the risk. If he saw us—or even suspected anything—he would make a scene. And I didn't want you caught in that mess." She paused.

"I was trying to protect you, Glen. That's all."

He was silent on the other end, and for a moment, she worried he hadn't believed her. But then she heard a soft sigh.

"Stop overthinking everything," she told him, trying to lighten the mood. "You're cute, you know that?"

He chuckled softly. "You're a bully," he teased.

She smiled at the sound of his grin. The tension between them eased, and things slowly returned to their usual rhythm. She promised him that they'd find time—real-time—and that she would make it up to him. He didn't argue.

The days passed, and Yolaine and Glen kept in touch regularly. They flirted, exchanged teasing messages, and shared moments over video calls when they could steal the time. With Glen, Yolaine felt alive again. She felt desired.

At home, she played the dutiful mother. She spent her evenings with Kaley, helping with homework, reading bedtime stories, and watching her daughter drift to sleep. But once Kaley was settled, Yolaine's thoughts often drifted to Glen. Late at night, curled up in bed with her phone, they would talk until the early hours.

As for Pierce… his presence in the house was more of a formality than anything. He was busy with work, often away on business, and when he was home, he kept his distance. A part of him seemed to understand that Yolaine needed space—but that wasn't out of respect for her feelings. It was guilt.

A few weeks earlier, Yolaine had caught him cheating. Again. It hadn't been his first affair. While he was working in Denmark, he'd had live-in lovers, long-term relationships he'd kept hidden for years. And even now, despite his promises, he was involved with another woman. He denied it, of course. Lied to her face with practised ease. But Yolaine knew better. She always knew.

Yet, she stayed. For Kaley. For appearances. But her heart had moved on.

#8
# When Desire Rules

It had been days and weeks since their last meaningful interaction. Though they'd been texting and calling, Glen gradually withdrew—a subtle hint that he longed to be with Yolaine in person. And Yolaine, ever perceptive, felt the growing distance between their digital exchanges and her yearning. She knew she had to bridge that gap. But how could they meet? Glen didn't live in the same city, and inviting him to her home would only raise questions about Pierce.

Just then, her mum rang. "Yolaine, could you come back home for a day or so? Rosie and Michael are in a huge row and on the brink of separation. You're the only one who can help sort this out."

The real reason she had been seeking an escape was simple—a way to leave the city without raising any suspicions, a legitimate excuse to be away for a while.

After a brief conversation with Pierce, who was far from convinced and insisted on accompanying her, she managed to persuade him otherwise. "I'll handle things quickly, and Kaley will enjoy spending time with my parents," she explained, making up excuses to justify her departure. It made sense for Rosie and Michael to live near her mother's house.

Early the next morning, she packed up and left with Kaley. Before she left, Yolaine quickly told Glen: *I'm coming over for a few days. I'd love it if you could find a way to join me.*

Glen hesitated for just a moment before replying. After some convincing from his parents, he secured permission. He then took his bike and rode nearly 100 miles to meet Yolaine.

Meanwhile, Yolaine reached her mum's house. It was almost noon. When she arrived, she settled Kaley and herself into the cosy atmosphere. Her mum, dad, and gran were already there, busy pampering Kaley and ensuring everything was in order. When Kaley heard that Glen—Yolaine's cousin—was coming over for a few days, her eyes lit up with excitement.

"Grandma, did you hear? Glen is coming!" she chirped, tugging at her gran's hand.

Her gran smiled warmly, "Oh, how lovely to have him with us again."

As the evening went on, Yolaine took a moment to text Glen again. *So, are you on your way? I can't wait to see you.*

A few minutes later, her phone buzzed with his reply. *Yes, I'm almost there. I can't wait to catch up.*

Yolaine felt a flutter of anticipation. Amid the familiar hum of family life—her mum and dad discussing the latest family drama, Kaley chattering excitedly about the arrival of her cousin—Yolaine couldn't help but smile to herself. This was more than just a casual meeting; it was an opportunity to reconnect on her terms, away from the prying eyes at home.

Soon enough, the doorbell rang. Yolaine's heart skipped a beat. She exchanged a knowing glance with her gran before answering the door. There stood Glen, slightly dishevelled from his long journey but wearing that familiar, hopeful smile.

"Glen," she breathed, stepping forward.

"Yolaine," he greeted warmly, his voice low and sincere.

The atmosphere between them was charged with quiet excitement as they embraced briefly, silently acknowledging the significance of this secret reunion. Inside, conversation flowed easily—a mix of playful banter and deep, unspoken understanding that only family could share.

"I managed to convince my parents to let me come," Glen said, rubbing the back of his neck sheepishly. "I couldn't let you have all the fun without me."

Yolaine laughed softly. "I'm glad you're here. It's been too long."

As they settled into quiet conversation in the warm glow of her mum's bedroom, the burdens of the past few days seemed to melt away—replaced by the promise of a secret rendezvous that could heal more than just strained family ties.

Yolaine's mum began discussing the ongoing issues between Rosie and Michael, confessing that she hated involving Yolaine in their quarrels. "I had no choice," she sighed. "Rosie and you have been cousins since childhood."

Yolaine grinned and replied, "It's no trouble at all that you've involved me—in fact, I'm happy to help," she said, glancing at Glen and giving him a playful wink.

Glen returned the grin, then said, "I know I'm the youngest in the house, but I reckon all this happened because they didn't follow the tradition of not seeing the bride and groom before the ceremony."

Yolaine burst out laughing. "That's just a tradition—do you believe in that?"

Her mum interjected, "Yes, it should be followed. I wonder why this generation doesn't uphold tradition."

Yolaine's father remained silent, fully aware that any further comment might set off a flare-up.

Then Yolaine announced, "I'm going tomorrow morning to meet Rosie and Michael. I've told them I'm coming over to talk—maybe I can help sort things out."

As it turned out, Michael was quite pleased to hear that she was coming. He welcomed the prospect of speaking with his closest cousin, hopeful that Yolaine might be the one to help resolve their troubles.

"The discussion then diverted into other gossip, and they laughed and joked. Later, Yolaine decided to head into town, taking Kaley and Glen with her—she wanted to spend quality time with her cousin. There was no suspicion within the family; spending time with cousins was as natural as breathing."

They strolled through the streets, window shopping and meandering through the lively market. They stopped for ice cream and later enjoyed a cosy dinner at a small, inviting café. As the evening deepened and the sky turned dark, they finally went home.

Back at the house, Yolaine's mum, dad, and gran sat on the porch, chatting and enjoying the cool night air. Yolaine, Glen, and Kaley joined them, and soon, laughter and playful banter filled the porch. After a while, it was time to put Kaley to bed. Yolaine took her daughter inside, and soon, the adults began to retire—mum, dad, and gran heading to their respective bedrooms.

Glen was given a makeshift bed in the living room. Meanwhile, Yolaine remained in her bedroom, her heart fluttering as she recalled the pleasant moments of the evening. Waiting in the living room, Glen was both excited and nervous; it had been weeks since they'd had a chance to spend time together like this. Their secret bond rekindled on a simple night out, now hummed with the promise of more shared moments.

After putting Kaley to bed—a process that took longer than expected—Yolaine finally emerged into the quiet living room. She was wearing a silky black nightdress that made her look utterly enchanting. Glen's eyes widened as he took her in; she looked like a dream made real.

They sat on the couch, talking about trivial, general matters—the conversation that belied the electric tension between them. Yolaine knew her mum and dad would likely retire soon, though there was always the chance they might wander out later, which could jeopardise their precious time alone. Hoping for a peaceful night, she squeezed out every moment of conversation with Glen.

After a while, as the house grew quieter and the soft hum of the night settled in, Yolaine rose from the couch. Reaching over, she gently took Glen's hand and led him towards her bedroom.

Lucky for Yolaine, her family always kept her room untouched whenever she returned—no one was allowed to use it in her absence. She'd arranged for Kaley to sleep in a cosy corner of the bed, ensuring her daughter was safe and sound.

With a secret smile and a subtle, knowing glance, Yolaine ushered Glen into her private sanctuary, where the night's unspoken promises awaited —her bedroom, a space reserved solely for her return, untouched by anyone else. She deliberately closed the door behind them and clicked the lock, sealing out the world. The room was bathed in a soft, amber glow from a single bedside lamp, its light accentuating every curve of her body and how her silky black nightdress clung to her form.

Glen's eyes darkened with desire as he stepped closer. His hands reached out, trembling slightly, and he lifted her nightdress with measured care. The fabric slid slowly from her shoulders, pooling at her waist to reveal the smooth expanse of her bare skin. His gaze dropped lower, and with a surge of heat, he noted that she wasn't wearing her panties on purpose—she knew he adored seeing her unadorned, a daring omission that only fanned the flames of his desire.

Yolaine met his gaze in a silent challenge as his fingertips traced along her collarbone, sending shivers cascading down her spine. Their kisses, soft at first, quickly deepened into a searing, hungry exchange. Each kiss, each caress became an exploration, as if they were rediscovering one another after a long, agonising separation.

With a gentle urgency, Yolaine guided him to the bed. There, beneath the cool sheets, their passion grew with each lingering touch. Glen's hands roamed over her bare breasts, cupping them tenderly before his lips descended in a slow, deliberate kiss over her sensitive nipples. Yolaine arched her back, a soft moan escaping her as his tongue flicked teasingly over her hardened nipples, sending pulses of pleasure through her.

Not content to merely worship her curves, Glen's hand slipped lower, caressing the smooth fold of her inner thigh. Yolaine's breath hitched when his fingers brushed against the heat of her skin, and she reached down, guiding him with a sultry look. Her hand found the base of his shaft, already throbbing with need, and she drew him closer. His skin glistened with anticipation in the low light as she traced delicate patterns along him.

Their intimacy was slow, every movement deliberate. Yolaine's lips trailed kisses down his neck, over his chest, until she returned her focus to his hard length. She took it into her mouth with a mix of tenderness and unbridled hunger, her tongue swirling around him as she savoured his taste. Glen's moans filled the room, his hands tightening in response as he succumbed to the waves of pleasure building within him.

For a moment, the world outside ceased to exist as Yolaine's attention shifted from his shaft to his balls. She alternated between soft, teasing kisses and gentle suckling, eliciting a symphony of velvety, desperate moans from him. The moment's intensity was palpable—every touch and whispered word heightened their shared heat.

Seeing his body tremble excitedly, Yolaine pulled back just enough to meet his gaze. "Relax, love," she murmured, her voice a soothing caress against his ear. "Let yourself feel this."

Encouraged by her whispered encouragement, Glen's desire surged anew. Yolaine pulled herself up from their shared embrace, then, eyes smouldering, moved beside him. Glen began exploring her anew in the soft amber glow of the bedside lamp. He started by kissing her tenderly along her neck, trailing slow, deliberate kisses onto her shoulder and chest. As he worked his way lower, he softly suckled on her breast, alternating between gentle, teasing kisses and firm, caressing suckles. His fingers deftly toyed with her nipples—squeezing one softly while his lips lavished attention on the other—eliciting quiet, breathless moans from her.

Then, Glen's kisses drifted further down her body. He traced a line from her chest to her belly, moving along the side of her hips and thighs with unhurried, almost reverent tenderness. When his lips reached the delicate inner thigh, Yolaine spread her legs deliberately, inviting him closer. Glen buried his face in the soft heat there, his tongue trailing over her folds. He licked slowly, tasting her with a measured intensity, then pushed his tongue deeper, exploring every secret contour.

Unable to contain the mounting heat, he slid a finger into her inviting fold. A soft moan escaped her as she shivered with pleasure. "Use two fingers, please," she whispered, her voice trembling with anticipation. Glen obliged, carefully inserting another finger while continuing his teasing lick. Their intimate rhythm built steadily—a symphony of soft moans, whispered names, and the wet sound of skin meeting skin.

Before long, Glen did something unexpected—he intensified his efforts, tongue moving with renewed urgency as he delved deeper into her desire. Yolaine gasped, her body arching in response as she guided him further, her hands trembling with both passion and need.

Unable to hold back any longer, she pulled him upward and whispered, "Come up and take me." Glen shifted, aligning himself with her in a slow, deliberate motion. With controlled intensity, he began to thrust into her, each movement deep and measured at first, then building in fervour as the night's passion took hold. Yolaine spread her legs wider, drawing him in completely, and as he entered her fully, she wrapped her legs around his waist. Their movements grew increasingly intense—slow and burning, then quick and insistent—each thrust a desperate reclaiming of the time they feared might never come again.

Between heated kisses, Yolaine clung to him, and Glen's hand found her breast once more, drawing it into his mouth as he continued his passionate pace. "I can't bear it," he murmured between kisses. "May I come?"

"Yes, sweetheart," she replied huskily. "We have all night—do as many times as you want."

With that, Glen's rhythm shifted once more. He quickened his pace, their bodies moving together in a tempest of desire until he finally reached his peak, his body shuddering as he exploded within her. For long moments afterwards, they lay entwined, skin slick with sweat and shared satisfaction, their breaths coming in soft, ragged gasps. The room remained hushed in the aftermath, their intense connection lingering in every whispered sigh and tender caress—a secret promise of more stolen moments in the dark.

They lay side by side, entwined in a gentle embrace, their skin still glistening with the remnants of their passion. Tender caresses and soft kisses punctuated the quiet moments as they whispered to one another, sharing secrets and sweet promises. Glen admired her with eyes full of wonder, and Yolaine returned his gaze with an equal measure of adoration, both lost in the intimate glow of their shared affection.

"Yolaine leaned to her left to check on Kaley, who was fast asleep. Then she turned back to Glen, her gaze deep and soulful. A playful glint danced in her eyes as she broke the lingering silence. 'Do you think you're up for round two?' she teased, her tone light but laced with invitation."

Glen's eyes lit up with mischief as he replied, "Oh, yes—but I want something different this time."

"Whatever you want," she murmured, a teasing smile on her lips.

After a moment's thought, he said, "I saw a film where a man picked up a woman and did it standing against a wall."

Yolaine laughed softly. "That's for chaps who are strong enough to lift a woman as if she were a feather."

"Then let me try," Glen challenged.

They slid off the bed and moved to a quiet corner near the wall. With determined effort, Glen squared his shoulders and attempted to lift Yolaine. He strained slightly, his muscles flexing as he tried to hoist her upward.

"You're stronger than you look—I must say," Yolaine teased, wrapping her legs around his waist as he steadied himself. With a slow, deliberate motion, Glen found her fold and pressed forward, eliciting a soft moan from her.

The room seemed to pulse with the building intensity of their daring experiment. Glen's standing thrusts, though unpolished and rough in their urgency, sent waves of ecstasy through Yolaine. Each powerful thrust made her breasts bounce enticingly, the sway of her curves an irresistible invitation. Her moans grew louder, echoing against the wall as Glen's movements became forceful and desperate.

"Can you be a bit rougher?" Yolaine gasped between kisses. "Thrust me deeper—make me feel every bit of you."

Glen's eyes darkened further with desire as he obliged, turning his movements into a series of sharp, controlled jerks. With each sudden, intense thrust, Yolaine yelped softly—a mixture of delight and exultation that spurred him on. Yet even as the intensity built to a fever pitch, Glen's strength met its limit; he could no longer sustain her weight in that upright position.

Realising their precarious balance, Glen slowly guided Yolaine away from the wall and back to the bed. Laying her down gently, he paused, his chest heaving, the heat of their passion still blazing in his eyes. Yolaine, catching her breath, reached up to kiss him tenderly—a soft, affectionate counterpoint to the earlier wildness.

"I know you were just trying to impress me," she murmured, a mischievous glint in her eyes. "But next time, we might have to stick to the bed."

Their laughter mingled with whispered promises as they lay together, their skin slick with sweat, the air heavy with the shared intensity of their union. In that private sanctuary, every touch had been an exploration and every moan a testament to their reawakened desire. This secret, intense connection promised more daring adventures in the coming nights.

But Yolaine wasn't finished with him. Not yet.

Her gaze held his, dark and luminous, a silent invitation that spoke of forbidden promise. A slow, knowing smile curved her lips as she leaned in close, her breath warm against his ear.

"Now," she whispered, voice low and velvety, "it's my turn."

She guided Glen back against the pillows with deliberate grace, her fingers tracing over his chest as though memorising every inch of him. There was no rush—no need for haste. They had time. Time to explore, linger, and lose themselves entirely in each other.

She straddled him slowly, her thighs framing his hips as she settled herself atop him, her body moving with elegant control. For a moment, she sat there, her hands resting lightly on his chest, feeling the steady rhythm of his heartbeat beneath her palms. She let the silence stretch, drawing out the anticipation until Glen's breath hitched, his hands instinctively sliding up to rest on her hips.

Her fingers wrapped tenderly around him, guiding him to where she was already wet and ready. She didn't take him in at once—no. She teased herself with him, her body pressing down ever so slightly, letting him feel her heat, her slickness, before lifting again. The look in her eyes was both playful and deeply intimate.

"Feel that?" she murmured. "That's for you."

Finally, slowly, she lowered herself, inch by inch, until he was entirely inside her. A soft, broken sigh slipped from her lips as he filled her, stretching her most exquisitely. She stilled there, letting herself adjust, savouring the fullness, the way their bodies joined so perfectly.

Yolaine's movements were slow at first—achingly slow. Her hips rolled in a steady rhythm, a languid dance that made Glen's breath catch in his throat. His hands roamed her thighs, her waist sliding up to her breasts. She arched into his touch, encouraging him without words. His fingers found her nipples, teasing them in slow, lazy circles that made her shiver and moan softly.

She leaned forward, her hands bracing on his shoulders, her lips brushing against his in a tender and possessive kiss. Their mouths moved together unhurriedly, tasting, teasing, until she pulled away just enough to whisper, "You like this, don't you? Watching me take my time with you…"

Glen's answer was a low groan, his hips instinctively lifting to meet hers.

"I do," he murmured, his voice thick with desire. "I love every second of it."

Yolaine smiled, slow and sultry, and guided his hands back to her breasts, encouraging him to squeeze, to tease, to make her feel as cherished as he did. Her own hands wandered, tracing the lines of his arms and neck, then into his hair, threading through the soft strands as she moved above him, her pace still unhurried, savouring every moment.

And then she bent down again, offering him her breast. Glen took it into his mouth, his tongue circling her nipple before sucking gently, then with more urgency, as though he couldn't get enough. She gasped, her fingers tightening in his hair, her body clenching around him in response.

Still, she didn't rush. Still, she made it last.

She rode him like that for what felt like forever, her body fluid and graceful, a rhythm as old as time. She watched him beneath her—the way his hands trembled as he held her, the way his breath came in ragged gasps, the way his gaze never left hers, dark with awe and need.

"You're mine tonight," she whispered, leaning down to kiss him, slow and deep.

"All yours," he breathed against her lips. "Every part of me."

She felt his body tense beneath her, his release building fast now, and she smiled, kissing him again before whispering, "Don't hold back. Give it to me."

Glen groaned, his body arching as he spilt into her, his hands gripping her hips as if anchoring himself. Yolaine kept moving, slower now, coaxing him through it, not letting him go. She was so close, but she wanted him to feel everything first. She wanted him to know he was hers.

Then she let herself go, her climax washing over her like a tide, her body trembling as she called his name in a soft, breathless cry.

"Glen…"

Her body tightened around him as the pleasure broke her open, and she collapsed against his chest, their hearts pounding in unison.

For a long time, they stayed like that, tangled together, their bodies slick with sweat, their breaths mingling in the dark. Yolaine's fingers traced lazy patterns over his skin, memorising the feel of him. She kissed his jaw, throat, and lips, each touching a silent promise, though neither spoke it aloud.

Eventually, as the quiet settled around them, she whispered, "Do you want more... or are you done for the night?" Glen chuckled softly, his voice warm yet weary. "I'm done—for now." He grinned, adding, "Don't forget I drove 100 miles for you. It's been a tiring day."

She smiled, though something in her chest ached. "Get dressed," she said softly. "It's late. You should go before they wonder."

Reluctantly, Glen rose, dressing in silence. Before he left, he bent and kissed her one last time—soft, lingering, a goodbye that wasn't quite a goodbye.

Then he slipped out, leaving Yolaine lying there alone in the dark, her body sated but her heart… aching. She closed her eyes, breathing in the silence, holding onto the memory of him, of them.

For tonight, he was hers. And that was enough.

For now.

#9

# Between Family and Secrets

The early morning hush wrapped the room in a soft, silver-blue glow. Yolaine lay still, lost in the depths of sleep, her breathing steady and slow. Just before sunrise, she stirred faintly at the warm weight of an arm sliding gently around her waist. A familiar presence. A quiet breath against her neck. Then, a tender kiss, barely there, followed by a playful nibble at her ear.

She turned slowly, already knowing who it was. Her dark lashes fluttered open to find Glen gazing at her, his eyes soft yet filled with something more profound. She offered him a sleepy, knowing smile before brushing her lips against his in a warm and longing kiss.

"You couldn't stay away, could you?" she murmured against his mouth, her voice still husky with sleep.

He smiled a crooked grin that always managed to stir her. "I had to see you... before the sun rose before the house wakes."

"Did you lock the door?" she asked softly, though she knew the answer.

"Yes," he whispered, as if sharing a secret just for her.

Kaley was tucked beside Yolaine, her slim body warm and sleeping peacefully. Carefully, Yolaine shifted her, placing a pillow at her side to keep her safe at the edge of the bed. Then she turned back to Glen, her gaze playful, a teasing glint in her dark eyes. "What am I going to do with you?" she whispered, fingers tangling gently in his tousled hair. "You're such a devil... but you're rather sweet."

He chuckled low, his fingers tracing the line of her jaw. "You could let me have an early breakfast," he said, his tone playful but laced with intent.

Yolaine's lips curved. "Greedy boy," she teased, catching his face in her hands and kissing him deeply. Her body warmed under his touch, and she didn't resist as his hands slid lower, finding the hem of her nightdress and lifting it slowly, reverently. He slipped her panties down with gentle care, his fingertips grazing her skin and sending shivers along her spine.

She lay back against the bed, her breathing already unsteady as he rose just enough to rid himself of his trousers. His need for her was evident—hard and ready—and she opened herself to him, legs parting with quiet invitation.

He entered her slowly, carefully, his gaze never leaving hers as he did. A soft sound escaped her throat, more of a gasp than a cry, as he filled her. She wrapped her legs around his waist, hands firm on his hips as if to keep him close, to keep him there, joined to her.

Their rhythm was slow at first, unhurried. She met his every movement with her own, hips rising to greet him, fingers slipping to the small of his back. His mouth sought hers, stealing kisses between soft groans of pleasure. He breathed her in—the scent of her skin, the warmth of her breath, the softness of her lips.

When his mouth found her breast, she arched up for him, offering herself without hesitation. He took her nipple into his mouth, sucking gently, his tongue teasing her while his body moved deep within her. Yolaine's hands slid through his hair, holding him there as heat bloomed low in her belly.

She was utterly awake now, every nerve alight with the slow burn of their shared desire.

His pace quickened as he whispered, "I can't... I'm going to—"

She smiled, breathless, and drew him closer with her legs, "Good boy," she whispered. "Don't stop... take me."

And he did. He gave her everything as he shuddered against her, spilling himself into her with a quiet, desperate sound. Still, she held him close, stroking his back gently as he softened, resting his forehead on hers.

"You're always ready," she whispered when she found her breath again, tracing his jaw with her fingers.

"Only for you," he replied, his voice rough but tender. "I don't know why... you undo me."

They lay together for a while, skin to skin, their bodies slick with shared warmth. Time seemed to slow as they kissed softly and exchanged whispers neither would dare say in daylight.

But the world was beginning to wake.

"You should go," she whispered, though every part of her wanted to keep him there. Her fingers lingered on his cheek, memorising his warmth.

He kissed her softly, then rose. His movements were quiet as he dressed, glancing back at her one last time before slipping out the door.

Yolaine lay still for a moment, breathing in the scent of him that lingered on the sheets. Then, with a soft sigh, she rose and padded to the washroom. She cleaned herself carefully, the cool water refreshing against her heated skin. She took a moment, steadying herself, her reflection faint in the mirror.

When she returned to bed, she tucked herself in beside Kaley, who murmured in her sleep but didn't wake. Yolaine closed her eyes, exhaustion finally claiming her, though a faint, secret smile curved her lips as she drifted back asleep.

Morning broke quietly over the house. Pale sunlight crept through the thin curtains, casting a soft glow across the wooden floors. The stillness didn't last long. Soon, the gentle murmur of voices and the clatter of utensils filled the air as Yolaine's mother and grandmother bustled about in the kitchen, preparing breakfast and tending to the usual household chores.

Yolaine stirred slowly from sleep, still warm from the night's memories. She sat up, took a deep breath, and ran a hand through her hair. Kaley was still curled up at the edge of the bed, sleeping soundly, undisturbed by the sounds from outside the room.

With quiet steps, Yolaine left the room and went to the kitchen. The air smelled of brewing tea and coffee. Her mother smiled briefly while her grandmother handed her a cup of warm water, as was their morning habit.

They chatted for a while, straightforward talk about the day ahead—who was coming, what needed to be done—nothing out of the ordinary. Yolaine kept her tone light, hiding the tangle of thoughts beneath her calm exterior. After some time, she excused herself and went to the washroom. She closed the door gently behind her and washed up, the cool water a welcome contrast to the heat lingering beneath her skin.

Meanwhile, Glen was only stirring. He stretched lazily on the makeshift mattress in the living room's corner. After a long moment, he sat up, rubbing his eyes before rolling up his bedding and pushing it aside. He slumped onto the couch with a sleepy smile, still tugging at his lips.

Yolaine's mother brought him a cup of tea without a word. Glen accepted it with a grateful nod, offering her a warm smile. He sipped quietly, his eyes meeting hers briefly—searching, cautious, but polite.

Moments later, Yolaine's father emerged from his room, dressed and ready for the day. He settled into his usual spot in the living room and greeted Glen with a friendly nod. The two exchanged morning pleasantries, the conversation light and casual, as though nothing was amiss.

Later that morning, she got ready to visit Rosie and Michael. She slipped into a light dress and pinned her hair back neatly. Glen was sitting by the window then, watching her, and she was just about to ask if he wanted to come along when her mother spoke.

"I'll come with you," her mother said, wiping her hands on a dishcloth. "Let Glen stay here. We can manage on our own."

There was no room for protest in her voice. Yolaine hesitated momentarily, searching Glen's face, but he only gave a faint shrug. She forced a smile and nodded. "Alright."

Yolaine and her mother set out on foot. Rosie's house wasn't far—just a short walk from Yolaine's mother's home. The sun was already high in the sky, and the neighbourhood was quiet, the stillness hanging thick in the warm air. They walked in silence at first, their footsteps steady on the dirt path.

Then her mother spoke.

"I hope you know what you're doing," she said quietly as if testing the weight of her words.

Yolaine felt her chest tighten, the leisurely morning slipping away instantly. She glanced at her mother, searching her face. "What do you mean?" she asked, calm but unsure.

Her mother didn't look at her. Her gaze remained fixed ahead, her voice steady and unyielding. "I know."

Those two words hit harder than anything Yolaine had expected. Her stomach churned, her breath catching in her throat. For a moment, she couldn't find the words. Her thoughts raced, but they all led to one undeniable truth— her mother had found out.

"I... I don't understand," Yolaine tried again, though her voice wavered.

Her mother stopped walking and turned to face her; her expression etched with something that wasn't quite an anger but wasn't forgiveness. She spoke quietly, "I saw Glen leaving your room."

Yolaine felt the world tip beneath her feet. The fear she'd been holding at bay flooded her, hot and sharp. She couldn't speak. Her mother waited, her gaze unwavering.

But Yolaine stayed silent.

They continued walking the rest of the way without another word, each step heavy with unspoken tension. Yolaine's heart pounded, not for herself, but for Glen. She feared for him, for what this revelation could mean for his future. He was young, still with so much ahead of him. She had already made her mistakes.

Her mother's silence spoke volumes, more than any words could. She knew. And there was no taking it back now.

When they arrived at Rosie's house, Yolaine breathed deeply to steady herself, smoothing her dress with trembling hands before knocking on the door.

But her mind remained back on that path, with the weight of her mother's knowing gaze pressing down on her chest. She knew there was no point in making excuses or defending herself. Her mother had seen the world, and she could easily discern what was happening. For now, all Yolaine wanted was to protect Glen.

Rosie greeted them warmly at the door, her smile radiant as she welcomed them inside. "It's so lovely to see you both!" she said, her voice warm and sincere. Michael, standing a little apart, was equally polite, offering a nod of greeting. His expression was pleasant, though there was a subtle air of restraint, as though he understood the weight of the conversation that was about to unfold.

Without hesitation, Michael excused himself, giving Yolaine and her mother a small, understanding smile as he entered another room. He knew that Yolaine and her mother would likely need some time alone with Rosie to discuss the difficulties she and Michael were facing. As he left, Yolaine couldn't help but feel a strange blend of sympathy and concern for both of them.

Yolaine had known Rosie for most of her life. They were cousins, but their bond went far deeper than that. They were childhood friends, confidantes who had shared many secrets over the years. She also knew Michael, though not as closely. Rosie and Michael had been childhood sweethearts, their love story beginning long before their marriage. Yolaine was aware of the intimate history between them, a history that wasn't always as innocent as it seemed. There had been moments when Yolaine had stepped in to protect Rosie, covering for her when their secret moments threatened to be exposed.

One memory in particular flashed in Yolaine's mind. It was after the New Year's dance that Rosie and Michael wanted a private space to be alone. Rosie had turned to Yolaine for help. Eager and persistent, Michael had been pressuring Rosie for weeks, wanting to take their relationship to a more intimate level. Yolaine, the supportive cousin, had offered them the attic of her house as a sanctuary.

The house had been quiet when they returned home after the dance, Yolaine's parents and grandmother deep in sleep. Yolaine had tiptoed around the house, careful not to wake anyone, before leading Rosie and Michael to the attic. The soft moonlight filtered through the window, casting a dim glow on the room. She had switched on the light in the attic, illuminating the space. A rug lay on the floor, and Michael was all over Rosie before they had settled.

"Hold on," Yolaine whispered, her voice barely audible. Let me go downstairs first." Rosie grinned mischievously while Michael, momentarily embarrassed, blushed. Yolaine stood guard downstairs, hoping her family wouldn't stir during the night, while her thoughts raced as she could hear the muffled sounds of their passion above.

Curiosity had gotten the better of her, and Yolaine had quietly crept back up the stairs to peek at what was happening. In the faint light, she had seen

Rosie sitting on Michael's lap, his body arched back in pleasure as he kissed her and caressed her. Rosie was riding him slowly, their passion more intense than Yolaine had expected. The sight was exciting and overwhelming, and she had quietly retreated downstairs, unsure what to think or feel.

Later, when Rosie and Michael descended from the attic, they left without saying a word. Rosie gave Yolaine a knowing grin, and Michael drove her home before leaving. Yolaine, deep in thought, had realised something crucial about relationships—the heart of the tension between Rosie and Michael lay in communication and unspoken expectations.

Once they were all settled in Rosie's living room, Yolaine's mother sat quietly on the other side, offering Yolaine space to talk with Rosie. Yolaine knew that her mother was there more as an observer than a participant, understanding that only Rosie and Michael could genuinely work through their issues. No amount of external advice would resolve what was happening between them.

After a long silence, Rosie finally spoke, her voice heavy with frustration. "It's just not working, Yolaine," she admitted. "Michael doesn't help with the housework. I struggle to balance my job and the house, and he doesn't seem to understand. We don't talk enough; we don't connect. And… then there's the intimacy. He expects it every day, and he wants even more on weekends. But I'm just exhausted. I don't feel like it."

Before Yolaine could respond, Michael stepped out of the room, his face tense from having overheard the conversation. "She doesn't give me space," he interjected, his voice sharp. "She expects me to start doing housework as soon as I walk through the door. I don't get to relax."

The atmosphere in the room became thick with tension as Rosie and Michael started to argue, their voices rising. Yolaine listened carefully, her thoughts swirling as she tried to think of the right words. Meanwhile, her mother remained silent on the other side, watching with an expression that was both knowing and resigned. She understood, as Yolaine did that only Rosie and Michael could resolve their issues, but it was clear that their communication had broken down.

Yolaine, wanting to offer something more, shared her own experience. "I understand," she said softly. "I've been through a lot myself, especially with Pierce. Things were fine at first, but then I discovered his infidelity. I was pregnant with his child by then, so I gave him another chance. We're trying to work things out, but it's hard. Life is a rollercoaster. You're both newly married and adjusting to living together can be challenging. But it's something you have to work through together. No one else can fix it for you."

She paused, her voice steady but tinged with emotion. "If you think space is needed, maybe take a break. Go on a holiday, try to reconnect, and rediscover each other. Separation isn't the answer for a loving couple like you two. Marriage is about give and take. You win some, you lose some."

Rosie and Michael exchanged a look, their tension easing slightly. After a moment, Rosie nodded, her expression softening. "We'll give it a try," she said quietly. "We know you care, Yolaine." To break the ice, Michael suggested, "How about we all have dinner together soon? We're unsure when we'll meet again, but we'd love to have everyone together."

Yolaine smiled, feeling a slight weight lift. It wasn't a perfect solution, but it was a start. They had acknowledged the difficulties in their relationship, and for now, that was enough.

Before leaving, Rosie approached Yolaine and thanked her sincerely for coming over. "Thank you for being here, Yolaine. I appreciate your support," she said, her voice filled with gratitude.

Yolaine smiled; her words were soft but genuine. "I'm glad to be of help," she replied. "And honestly, you did me a big favour by calling me to help you."

Rosie paused, her brow furrowing in confusion. She wasn't sure what Yolaine meant by that. Yolaine's smile remained, though her voice had a quiet, reflective tone.

Yolaine had been looking for an excuse to come over, a way to escape the tension of her own life. Being with Glen felt like fresh, unique, authentic air. It had been a relief to be with him, to feel something different from the complications Pierce had caused. But now, with her mother's awareness of the situation, things felt uncertain. Her mother knew, and Yolaine couldn't shake the feeling that everything was about to change.

# #10
# The Weight of Secrets and Goodbyes

Yolaine and her mother arrived home, and the familiar hum of their household was greeting them as they stepped inside. Glen was in the living room, playing with Kaley, his laughter filling the air, while Yolaine's father watched them with a content smile. Yolaine's grandmother was busy in the kitchen, the scent of her cooking drifting through the house.

Yolaine didn't immediately approach Glen. Instead, she padded to her bedroom, avoiding him as she tried to gather her thoughts. Her mother, oblivious to what had transpired, continued with her usual warmth, going to the kitchen to help her mother without a hint of suspicion. The normalcy of the scene felt almost suffocating to Yolaine. It was as if the weight of her secret had grown unbearable.

Dinner came and went, the evening unfolding as it always did. The family sat around the table, laughing and joking, carrying on as though everything was fine. Later, they all retired to their usual spots—Glen preparing his makeshift bed in the living room, his anticipation palpable. He waited for Yolaine, expecting her to come to him as always.

After putting Kaley to bed, Yolaine went to the living room. She sat on the couch, but Glen immediately noticed something was off. She wasn't herself—distant, quiet, almost too calm. He sensed something was wrong but couldn't quite grasp it.

"Yolaine, what's going on?" he asked, his voice laced with concern. "You've been acting strange all day."

She motioned for him to sit beside her. As he did, her gaze met his, her face serious. "Glen, my mum knows about us," she said softly.

The words hit him like a punch to the gut. His eyes widened in shock, and he couldn't speak for a moment. Fear gripped him, and he felt a cold sweat across his forehead. He knew the complications this could bring. Her mother and his mother were closely related, and the last thing he wanted was for this to escalate between the families.

"I have to leave," Glen stammered, his voice trembling. "I can't stay here. What if this gets worse? What if my mum finds out?"

Yolaine reached out to calm him, her hand gently resting on his. "Glen, don't panic," she said firmly. "This won't go any further. It won't reach our mothers, I promise. We'll figure this out, but you have to stay calm."

But Glen was panicking. He was inexperienced in dealing with this pressure, and his mind raced with worst-case scenarios. Yolaine could see the fear in his eyes and knew she couldn't leave him like this. He might do something drastic, or worse, he could leave the house in the middle of the night. She couldn't let that happen, not to him, not because of her.

She felt a pang of guilt. Glen was the last person she wanted to hurt, and now he was caught in a mess she had created. With a deep sigh, she took his hands and guided him gently to her bedroom. "Come on," she said softly, locking the door behind them once they were inside.

Kaley was sound asleep, and the room was quiet and still. Yolaine sat down on the bed, pulling Glen beside her. She placed his hands in hers and looked at him thoughtfully. "You're staying here tonight," she said, her voice strong and resolute. "Tomorrow, we'll figure this out. But for now, relax. You're not leaving. Everything's going to be fine."

Glen's head, the panic still visible in his eyes, but he trusted her. Yolaine was always strong and knew how to handle situations like this. Slowly, he nodded, allowing himself to relax, if only a little. He lay down beside her, still shaken but feeling the slightest bit of comfort in her presence.

Yolaine kept her eyes on him, reassuring him with her calm, steady gaze. She would handle this. She would ensure things didn't spiral out of control for his sake.

As she helped him settle into the bed, her gaze softened. She was determined to ease his mind and make him feel safe in her presence. She kissed his shoulder, her lips lingering there for a moment, whispering reassurances in a soothing tone. Her touch was gentle but firm, offering the comfort he desperately needed. The hours passed in silence, save for the quiet rustling of the sheets and the soft, steady rhythm of their breaths.

Yolaine remained awake, her eyes never leaving him as he began to calm. She watched him closely, her heart swelling with both concern and affection. He seemed more at peace now, his body relaxing under her touch, and she let out a quiet breath of relief. Slowly, she leaned in and kissed the nape of his neck, her lips soft against his skin. She could feel his warmth and the steady beat of his pulse beneath her touch.

As the night deepened, a quiet, unspoken desire passed between them. He turned to face her, their eyes locking in a silent exchange. Without a word, their lips met—slow and tender—filled with the weight of their emotions. It was a moment that neither of them could deny, where everything else in the world faded away. She kissed him back, her heart racing, the connection between them undeniable.

When his gaze met hers again, something deep and unspoken passed between them. His eyes darkened with desire, and she felt the undeniable pull of it. Without a word, he reached for her, his lips capturing hers in a kiss that was soft yet filled with longing. She kissed him back, the intensity of their connection surging with every passing moment as if the world itself had disappeared.

Her hands roamed over his chest, feeling the heat of his skin beneath her fingertips. His body was solid and warm, and as her hands traced the lines of his muscles, she could feel his heart racing. She kissed him again, this time moving lower to his neck, feeling the steady pulse beneath her mouth. His breath hitched, and she felt his body respond, groaning softly at the gentle caress of her lips.

Yolaine slowly pulled away, her eyes locking with his, and her fingers moved to the waistband of his pants. With a soft, teasing smile, she unbuttoned them slowly, her fingers brushing against the growing hardness beneath. His breath quickened as she eased them down, exposing the stiff shaft that had been straining beneath the fabric. She paused momentarily, her eyes roaming over him, savouring the sight of his need.

She leaned down, placing soft kisses along his torso, her lips trailing lower, her breath warm against his skin. Her fingers gently wrapped around him, teasing him with light strokes, feeling his pulse under her touch. She watched him intently as she moved her hand up and down, the tension building between them with each soft caress. He groaned, his body reacting to her, urging her on, but she slowed, savouring the moment, giving him just enough to feel the heat but not the release.

"Yolaine," he murmured, his voice thick with desire, his hands reaching for her, but she stopped him with a gentle touch.

"Patience," she whispered, her voice thick with hunger. Slowly, she sat back up, her fingers trailing over her skin as she reached for the straps of her nightdress. She pulled them down slowly, teasingly, letting the fabric fall from her shoulders, revealing the curve of her breasts and the soft lines of her body. Her skin glowed in the dim light, and she felt his gaze burn through her, his eyes drinking in every inch of her.

She let the dress fall to the floor, standing before him in all her naked beauty. She moved closer, her body pressed against him as she kissed him again, her lips lingering on his. Her hands moved to his shirt, easing it off his shoulders, then trailing her fingers over his chest, moving lower to plant soft kisses on his nipples. She kissed him again before slowly easing his pants completely off, leaving him fully exposed to her touch.

She climbed over him, her body hovering above his as she guided him between her inner thighs, her touch gentle but firm. She looked into his eyes, her breath shallow, feeling the heat between them surge. "I want you," she breathed, her voice filled with longing. She positioned herself above him, her body trembling as she slowly lowered herself, feeling him stretch her folds as she took him completely.

The sensation was overwhelming, her body adjusting to his fullness as she moved against him. She moaned softly, her hands gripping his shoulders as she began to ride him slowly, savouring the deep, intimate connection. The tension between them built, every thrust sending waves of pleasure through her body as she moved in perfect rhythm with him. She kissed him again, her lips hungry for his, her body urging him deeper, faster.

He groaned, his hands moving to her breasts, his fingers teasing her hardened nipples as her body responded to his touch. She gasped, the pleasure building inside her as her body rocked against his. "You feel so good," he whispered, his voice ragged with desire, and she moaned in response, her body trembling as she moved with more urgency.

She moved her breasts toward his face and offered them to him as she kept riding him, her body trembling with the sensations. He kissed and sucked her breast, squeezing her nipple as she moaned loudly. "All yours," she gasped, her voice thick with need. "Have me more; I'm feeding my breasts to you... they are yours." She pressed them harder to his face, urging him on.

He lost control, ravaging her breasts with fervour, and with his other hand, he squeezed them more urgently, each squeeze sending another shiver of pleasure through her.

The passion between them grew more intense, and as she guided him with her movements, she felt the wave of pleasure building inside her, the heat of it threatening to overtake her. She leaned down to kiss him again, her body moving faster now, her breath quickening as the pleasure mounted. Her release was so close, and she could feel him, too, the tension in his body matching her own.

"Are you close?" she whispered against his lips, her voice low with longing.

He groaned in response, his pace quickening. "So close," he muttered.

With a final, deep thrust, he groaned loudly, his body trembling as he spilt his heat inside her. The feeling of him filling her sent her over the edge, and she cried out, her body trembling in his arms as they both reached the peak together. They stayed locked together, their bodies shaking with the aftershocks of their release.

Breathless and spent, Yolaine rested her head on his chest, her body still humming with the lingering sensations of their love. She could feel his heartbeat steady beneath her, and as they lay together in the quiet aftermath, she whispered, "That was everything."

He kissed her forehead softly, his hands gently stroking her back. "And so much more," he replied, holding her close.

They lay beside each other, the room filled with the soft sound of their breathing. The night felt timeless, as though it had stretched beyond reality, and in that stillness, they looked at each other—eyes locked in a tender gaze as if memorizing the very essence of each other. The silence was complete with unspoken words, filled with the weight of everything they had shared.

His hand gently moved to her face, brushing a stray lock of hair behind her ear. His touch was tender as if every motion was meant to keep this moment safe as if time itself might slip away if they didn't hold on to it long enough. She closed her eyes briefly, savouring the warmth of his touch against her skin, feeling the love and care in every caress.

Yolaine opened her eyes again, her gaze meeting his, the intensity of the night still alive between them. She reached out, her fingers lightly tracing the line of his jaw, moving slowly over his skin as if memorizing every curve and contour. She wanted to remember him like this—vulnerable, with no words spoken, just the softness of their touch and the shared connection that ran more profound than anything they had said.

"Promise me," she whispered, her voice thick with emotion, "that you'll remember this." Her fingers continued their slow path, moving down his chest, across the faint scars and the warmth of his skin.

He nodded, his hand trailing over her shoulder and then down the soft curve of her arm. "I will," he murmured, his voice husky and the emotion clear in his eyes. "I'll remember everything."

A gentle ache in the air could only be born from knowing that the present might be all they had left. He shifted, bringing her closer, his arm wrapping around her in a protective embrace. She rested her head against his chest, the steady beat of his heart soothing her in a way nothing else could. He caressed her back, his fingertips tracing small circles, the rhythm slow, loving, and full of reverence.

She let out a soft sigh, content and at peace in his arms. Her hand moved over him, the feel of his skin under her palm as she traced his chest muscles, then down to his stomach, feeling his warmth and the strength of the body that had held her so closely. Her fingers brushed over his side, savouring their tender intimacy in that quiet moment.

They didn't need to speak; their gentle, explorative touches said everything. There was a sweetness to how they caressed each other as if every touch was an unspoken promise to hold onto this moment and never forget the feeling of being so close and connected.

"Is this how you want to remember me?" she asked softly, her lips grazing his chest as she spoke. She raised her gaze to meet his, her eyes filled with vulnerability.

"Yes," he answered, his voice barely above a whisper. "This is how I want to remember you—this closeness, this... tenderness." His thumb gently traced her collarbone, moving slowly, lovingly.

She smiled, the emotion settling deep in her chest. The night stretched on, and the two of them remained wrapped in each other's arms, caressing and whispering soft words in the quiet stillness of the room. There were no promises beyond this night or certainty about the future. But at that moment, they were all that mattered. Their hands explored, their bodies entwined in gentle caresses as if trying to hold onto the love they had shared for as long as the night would last.

And as the night carried on, neither of them wanted to let go. The feeling of being together, of simply being *here* with each other, was more than enough.

Yolaine gently pulled away from Glen, her hands brushing against his arm as she spoke with a tenderness that matched the moment's weight. "You should go back to sleep," she whispered, quiet but firm. Glen hesitated, the unspoken sadness between them hanging like a heavy cloud. Deep in his heart, he knew that moments like these—raw, real, and full of love—would never come again. This was it, a fleeting, beautiful love, short-lived yet intense.

He turned to face her, his eyes searching hers with an intensity she could feel deep within her. "Can you be mine?" he asked, his voice thick with the weight of his feelings. There was a vulnerability in his words, a plea that was both heart-wrenching and hopeful.

Yolaine took a deep breath, her heart aching as she looked at him, her love for him clear in every glance, every movement. "I am yours," she replied softly, her voice trembling with emotion. "But," she continued, her eyes filled with tenderness and regret, "I wish my darling... But we have so many hurdles, so many challenges ahead."

Glen nodded, the reality of the situation settling in. He understood. It was the truth they both knew, yet the raw longing in his heart didn't easily fade. "I want you forever," he whispered, his voice filled with sincerity as if speaking the truth of his soul.

A small, sad smile tugged at Yolaine's lips. "I wish I could give that to you," she said, her voice soft but resolute. "But we can't wait for each other. We need to live our lives, separate paths, even though it hurts." She paused, her eyes meeting his with understanding. "You need to start over, Glen. Find someone who will love you the way you deserve. Someone who will want you as much as you want her."

The words hung between them, heavy with the unspoken love they shared. Glen looked down, nodding, understanding what she was saying. The weight of her advice hit him like a wave, but deep down, he knew she was right.

Yolaine noticed the glistening of tears in his eyes, and she reached out to him, pulling him into a warm embrace. Her arms wrapped around him, offering him the comfort she knew he needed. "We can meet whenever we can," she whispered. "But we can't wait for each other. We can't live in the past." She paused, pulling back just slightly to meet his gaze. "Go and start your life. You deserve to be happy."

Glen kissed her softly on the forehead, his lips lingering momentarily before pulling away. She noticed the silent tears that glistened in his eyes, and it broke her heart. Her own eyes watered, and they held each other in the silence of that moment, knowing that this goodbye, however soft, was inevitable.

But then, as Glen stood to leave, the door to their chapter closing, something inside Yolaine couldn't bear it. She couldn't watch him walk away without one more moment. Her heart ached as she grabbed his arm, pulling him back towards her. "Wait," she whispered, her voice breaking. "Please, just one more time. I want to feel you, feel your warmth. I want to remember this—remember you."

Glen looked down at her, his heart heavy with the same ache. He had already come to terms with it, but her words, the way she looked at him, made him falter. Slowly, he pulled his shirt over his head, his pants sliding down as he stood before her, their bodies bare of anything except the love and desire that had built over their time together.

Yolaine moved closer, her hands finding their way to his chest, her fingers trembling as she traced his skin. She held him tightly, pulling him back onto the bed, their bodies coming together once more. This time, it wasn't just about the physical—it was about everything they had shared and felt.

As they moved together, their connection was intense, filled with a passion stored in their hearts. The way their bodies intertwined and their hands roamed, every touch felt like an expression of everything they had been. It wasn't about desire alone—it was a final embrace of their love, giving each other something to remember when they couldn't be together anymore.

Their movements were slow at first, filled with reverence as if each second mattered. Yolaine whispered his name, almost like a prayer, as she held him close, their bodies trembling in unison. Every kiss was more than just a kiss—it was an unspoken promise of love, of what had been and what would never be again.

As they reached the peak together, the room seemed quiet, the world outside fading. Their bodies trembled, intertwined, holding onto each other as the wave of their shared release washed over them, culminating in everything they had experienced. For a moment, they were one—connected in a way that would remain in their hearts, even if they had to part.

When the silence fell, Yolaine rested her head on his chest, feeling his heartbeat slow beneath her. "Thank you," she whispered, her voice soft but full of love. "For everything."

Glen kissed the top of her head, his heart aching but full of something deeper. "You'll always be with me," he murmured, his arms holding her close, even though they both knew it was time to let go.

Glen left the room, the moment's weight lingering in the air. He moved slowly as though trying to shake off the emotions that still clung to him. His mind raced, but exhaustion soon took over, and he collapsed onto his bed. He tried to close his eyes, hoping to find some rest, but the night's events—the love they had shared, the goodbye—kept replaying in his mind.

Yolaine, on the other hand, couldn't sleep. Her thoughts were filled with Glen, how he had looked at her when they said their goodbyes, the rawness of their connection. She turned over on her side, the sheets tangled around her as she tried to find comfort. Her body ached, not just from the physicality of their final moments together but from the emotional weight of everything that had unfolded between them.

She could feel the lingering intensity of the night in her body. There were bruises on her breasts, a reminder of their desperate, passionate moments together. Her neck felt sore, the mark of his kisses still evident on her skin. She closed her eyes, touching her hand gently to her fold, feeling the tender ache where their bodies had once been locked in a final embrace. It was all so intense, so powerful, yet so fleeting.

Yolaine's heart felt heavy, and the loneliness of the moment started to settle in. She wanted to ensure this ended well for Glen and that their love didn't just fade into something unspoken and unresolved. She wanted him to find happiness, to start a new chapter—without her. She had said it earlier, but the weight of it now, as she lay there in the quiet of the night, hit her harder than before.

She sighed softly, turning again, her body tired but her mind restless. As much as she longed for peace, she knew this brief love had given them something special. Eventually, the emotional and physical toll of the night caught up with her. Her eyes fluttered shut, and slowly, despite her racing thoughts, sleep claimed her.

She drifted off into a dreamless slumber, her body still aching, but her heart, though heavy, was at least momentarily at peace.

Early the following day, the house was buzzing with activity. Everyone was in the kitchen, preparing breakfast or heading to wash up. Full of energy, Kaley jumped on Glen, who was still drowsy from the night before. Yolaine was still asleep, her peaceful face contrasting the lively atmosphere in the house.

Her mother entered the room and gently woke Yolaine, who groggily stretched before joining the others. The family gathered around the table, enjoying a warm breakfast together. However, the morning's comfort was bittersweet for Glen, who knew he would soon have to leave.

As Glen got ready to depart, Yolaine's grandmother, with a kind smile, told him to visit often. Her mother always graciously wished him well and reminded him to drive safely. "Please call us when you get home," she said warmly, "and do visit again soon. You'll always have a place here."

Yolaine's mother was a wise and understanding woman, mature beyond her years. While she recognised that her daughter was an adult capable of making her own choices, she still provided subtle support, aware of the complexities Yolaine was facing. She understood that Yolaine was struggling with her relationship with Pierce, offering empathy and insight without overtly interfering.

Yolaine, still feeling the heaviness of their time together, walked over to

Glen. Playfully, she ruffled his hair and called him a "duffer" with a teasing smile. "Keep in touch," she added, her voice softening, "you can always reach out to me. I'll be there for you."

Glen grinned, shaking his head. "I'm not the duffer you are!" he joked. "Wait till we meet again. I'll show you who's the real duffer." They both laughed, a comfortable moment of familiarity between them.

As he turned to leave, Yolaine whispered to him, "I love you. Please take care of yourself. Keep in touch... We'll always be together."

Glen looked back at her, his voice filled with affection. "I know," he said with a smile. "You can't get rid of me that easily." His lighthearted tone offered comfort, even if they both knew the truth was more complicated.

Yolaine, feeling a playful surge of mischief, whispered one more thing to him. "You know what? I'm not wearing panties," she said with a grin, her eyes sparkling with teasing.

Glen's smile widened, and he gave her a playful look. "You're not fair," he replied with a chuckle. "See you when I see you," he said, his voice warm, and he left.

As Glen walked away, Yolaine felt a deep sadness settle in her chest. She watched him leave, knowing it was the right choice for both of them, even though it hurt. She also understood the importance of keeping their situation private—she couldn't let Pierce find out. His reaction could bring trouble for Glen, and she was determined to prevent that. Yolaine had come to help resolve the issues between Rosie and Michael, hoping to save their marriage while spending time with Glen. What she hadn't expected was that this would end their connection. She knew it was too good to last, and they had no future. Her intention had been simple: to comfort Glen, who was struggling with his breakup, while also seeking warmth and companionship for herself. She never expected to become romantically involved with her cousin, someone she had always seen as family—an older cousin she had grown up with, played with, and shared childhood memories with.

Yolaine stayed for one more day, spending time with Kaley and the family before returning to her own home. Even as the days passed, she and Glen kept in touch, their conversations filled with playful flirting and heartfelt exchanges. But as time passed, the distance between them grew, and their once-close connection started to fade with the physical miles between them.

The Present

# Desire Untamed

Part II

#11
# Chossing Happiness

Yolaine sat across from Janice, her closest friend, as they talked about Yolaine's life and the past that had broken her, shaping her into someone she no longer recognised. It all came rushing back instantly, as though it had happened just yesterday. Eugene and Glen had always been her weaknesses. But there was a palpable tension in the air—Janice was trying to convince Yolaine to let go of Aston, her new lover, fearing that it would ultimately consume her. Janice had noticed the growing connection between them and was concerned it would ruin Yolaine's life, especially since it seemed to be driven entirely by the desire to get back at Pierce. Deep down, she knew this was the only possible reason behind it.

"You know, Yolaine, I understand that you're trying to rebuild things with Pierce, but… are you really okay with how things are going?" Janice asked, her voice soft but laced with concern. "You've been through so much, and I'm just worried you're not seeing things. I want what's best for you."

Yolaine sighed, her eyes drifting to the window as she gathered her thoughts. "I'm just trying to keep things together. For Kaley. For us. But it's hard, Janice. You know how many times I've given him chances... After everything with Eugene, I thought maybe Pierce could change. But he didn't. He promised me he would, but he lied again."

Janice nodded, understanding Yolaine's struggle all too well. "I get it. But letting go of Eugene wasn't easy either. You loved him, Yolaine. And now, with everything you've been through with Pierce, I don't want to see you lose yourself in this. You deserve more than this constant heartbreak."

Yolaine bit her lip, her gaze distant. "It wasn't easy, no. But when I left Eugene, I thought I could have a future with Pierce. I gave him another chance. And now look at us... He promised to change, but he went back to his old ways. That's why I went to stay at Mum's, trying to clear my head. And that's when I met Glen."

Janice raised an eyebrow, clearly concerned but not entirely surprised. "Glen? Your cousin? I suspected something when we were all at your mum's house, but I thought it was just a moment. You pulled away, didn't you?"

Yolaine nodded, her expression softening. "I did. It felt wrong. He's family, and he's young. I didn't want to complicate his life... or mine. But I needed someone, Janice. We both did. And even though it was brief, it gave me some clarity. It showed me that I couldn't keep hanging onto hope with Pierce. He promised to improve, but I'm not sure that's possible."

Janice listened intently, a hint of sadness in her eyes as she stayed silent. Yolaine continued, her voice tinged with frustration. "You know how that story ended. He went back to his old ways. And here I am again, stuck in a cycle with someone who doesn't change."

Yolaine leaned forward, her hands clasped together. "I won't let it break me again. I met someone else... Aston. He's training to be a priest, Janice. A man of faith. But despite that, we've started a relationship. It feels different. It feels real like there's no way out but in a good way."

Janice's eyes widened in surprise. "A priest? Really? Are you sure you know what you're getting into? You've already been through so much, and now this? I worry you might be jumping from one thing to another without dealing with the real issues."

"I'm not running from anything," Yolaine replied, her tone growing firmer. "I'm just trying to live my life on my terms. I can't keep pretending everything's fine when it's not. But you're right about one thing—Pierce has changed, but I know it won't last. He's too calculated, too set in his ways."

Janice shook her head softly, her concern growing. "I just don't want you to lose yourself in all of this, Yolaine. You're already so deep in it, and I fear it'll be too late before you realise you've forgotten who you are."

Yolaine paused, her gaze dropping to her hands, her fingers trembling slightly. "I know what I'm doing. I've thought about it a lot. But I need more than what Pierce can give me. More than this controlled intimacy, this fake connection. I need someone who understands me and who listens to me. Someone who wants to share my life—my real life."

As Janice and Yolaine were deep in conversation, the sound of the front door opening broke their moment. Pierce had returned from work, and the energy shift was immediate. Janice, sensing the change, quickly rose from her seat.

"I'll be off now. Think about what I said, Yolaine. Give it another try," she said, offering a quick but supportive smile.

Yolaine, a little distracted, nodded. "I will try." She gave Janice a small smile before walking her to the door.

As Janice left, Yolaine stood in the doorway momentarily, her thoughts swirling. The room felt charged, but she knew the conversation with Pierce was inevitable.

Pierce greeted Yolaine with a knowing look. He didn't need to ask; he could tell that something must have been brewing if Janice had been around for long. But Pierce said nothing, focusing instead on Kaley, who was outside playing. He knew she would be happy to have him home. The maid was busy in the kitchen, and with a simple nod, Pierce made his way upstairs to freshen up.

A few minutes later, Pierce returned downstairs, feeling the quiet in the house. Yolaine, however, seemed distant, her mind lost somewhere far away. He could feel the unease in the air, but he casually broke the silence instead of pressing her with questions. He leaned back in his chair, glanced at Yolaine, and said, "I've got to go out of town for a few days. What do you think about joining me and bringing Kaley along?"

Yolaine looked up, startled momentarily, her thoughts still far away. She paused, considering his words. "Out of town?" she asked, her voice soft.

"Yeah," Pierce replied, "I thought it might be a good change of pace for all of us." He tried to keep the tone light, though his eyes searched hers, hoping for a positive response.

Yolaine hesitated, feeling the weight of his suggestion pressing down on her. She didn't respond immediately; her mind was caught between the unspoken tension in their relationship and the idea of a fleeting escape. Would this be an opportunity to reconnect or another way to avoid confronting the truth? Pierce's gaze remained steady, his expression unreadable as he waited for her answer.

Reluctantly, Yolaine agreed to Pierce's suggestion. She knew him well enough to recognise the underlying motives but chose to play along for now. After all, he was her husband and the father of their child. But beneath the surface, Yolaine's resolve was unwavering. She would do whatever it took to find her happiness. She refused to continue being unthinkingly loyal and faithful when Pierce repeatedly broke her trust. She had no intention of leaving Aston for him, just as she had walked away from Eugene in the past. Glen had been a brief infatuation, a moment of comfort during a weak time—a friend she would always hold dear but someone with a brighter future she didn't want to complicate.

Yolaine had made a decision. She would adopt the same approach Pierce had used on her all these years. She would no longer be the woman who clung to hope and loyalty when neither had been returned.

The following day, they packed their bags and left for a long drive to a beautiful resort. One thing Yolaine had always admired about Pierce was his ambition. He thrived on the high life, always striving to lead a luxurious lifestyle and provide the best for Yolaine and Kaley. She had access to whatever she wanted—anything was hers to indulge in, with no cost spared.

But there was a cold, calculating side to Pierce behind all the luxury and comfort. He always wanted things his way, and his words were final. In their relationship, Yolaine had long since recognised the absence of emotional warmth, replaced by a hollow power struggle. He was good in bed, but his interest in her began to wane as the days passed. The passion had diminished, mainly because he had tasted life elsewhere, and now Yolaine was no longer the woman he desired. She was his wife, the mother of their daughter, Kaley, but the spark had faded.

Pierce and Kaley spent the day together at the resort, enjoying the swimming pool and the beach. Their laughter echoed as they moved from one activity to another. Kaley was carefree, drawing Pierce into her playful energy while he seemed to relax, enjoying the day. They swam side by side, joked about the waves, and shared stories as they strolled along the shore. Kaley focused entirely on Pierce, her gaze lingering on him with a sense of comfort and connection. On the other hand, Pierce occasionally glanced at Yolaine, who sat nearby, watching them, though she seemed distant, lost in her thoughts.

Yolaine, despite being physically present, found herself feeling unsettled. Something had shifted between her and Pierce, and she couldn't help but notice how he seemed more at ease with Kaley. She tried to shake off the feeling, telling herself that she was overthinking things, but deep down, she couldn't ignore the gnawing suspicion that Pierce's affections were no longer the same.

"Are you alright?" Pierce asked her, sensing the shift in Yolaine's mood. Yolaine quickly smiled, masking her discomfort.

"I'm fine, just enjoying the sun," she replied, though the tension in her voice was hard to hide.

As evening came, they got ready and exited their hotel room for dinner. The atmosphere was intimate, and the soft lighting and the gentle hum of conversation around them made for a relaxing evening. Pierce and Kaley were engaged in a lively discussion, their eyes locked, laughter shared between them. Yolaine, sitting across from them, found herself feeling increasingly isolated. The connection she once felt with Pierce disappeared, replaced by the easy chemistry between him and Kaley. Yolaine tried to focus on the meal, but the knot in her stomach grew tighter every moment.

When dinner had ended, they returned to their room. Once warm and comfortable, the space felt cold and distant, as if the air had turned heavy. Yolaine lay in the vast king-size bed, her body sunk into the softness of the mattress, but her mind was miles away, tangled in questions she couldn't answer. She had hoped—no, expected—that Pierce might seek her out after the intimacy they had once shared so effortlessly.

But instead, Pierce went to Kaley. The two of them settled into the bed, their laughter and soft words filling the air between them, leaving Yolaine on the far side, alone with her swirling thoughts.

Her mind raced. *Why hadn't he come to her?* she wondered; why *Kaley tonight?* The room's quiet was suffocating, amplifying the doubts and the unease gnawing at her heart. She turned her face to the wall, the coldness of it pressing against her cheek, while the weight of her confusion settled deeper into her chest. The day's warmth now seemed a distant memory, replaced by an unbearable silence that deepened her uncertainty.

*For just a moment, she thought she could give it one more try. If Pierce had approached her, she would have let him in, surrendered to whatever intimacy he offered, perhaps even hoping for the connection they had once shared.* But there, on the other side of the room, was the reality that he had chosen Kaley—his daughter—over her. The woman he had once promised to love. The choice felt like an echo of everything that had gone wrong between them.

Yolaine closed her eyes, her breath shaky, as she felt the distance between them stretch further, a space that seemed impossible to close. She would have given herself to him, but Pierce had chosen not to. And that, more than anything, left her feeling hollow and adrift in the quiet of the night.

#12

# Beneath the Surface

In every love affair, misunderstandings, jealousy, small hurts, and constraints lead to complicated situations. These often surface, and more often than not, they create havoc in relationships built on affairs and deceptions. This was precisely what had unfolded in this case, or at least that's what it looked like.

The following morning, very early, Yolaine was awoken by the sound of a hotel room door swinging shut. Startled, she glanced around the room, her eyes settling on Kaley, who was still fast asleep on the bed next to hers. Kaley had spent the night with Pierce, as he wanted to be with Kaley, their beloved and only daughter. Pierce had thoughtfully arranged a few pillows around her, ensuring she wouldn't fall from the bed.

Yolaine's mind raced with confusion, a sense of unease washing over her. Something wasn't quite right. Without hesitation, she grabbed her phone and immediately called Pierce. The phone rang but went unanswered. She tried again, then a third time, but still no response. Frustration and worry settled in her chest. *Where could he have gone?* She wondered.

Her curiosity and discomfort got the better, and she quickly dressed, deciding to find Pierce herself. She quietly slipped out of the hotel room, careful not to disturb Kaley. As she made her way down the corridor, her heart pounded. She didn't want to leave Kaley alone in the room, but she took the risk, knowing Kaley was still fast asleep. She promised herself she would return swiftly, but she needed to understand why Pierce had left so early in the morning and, more importantly, why he wasn't responding to her calls.

She stepped into the lift and pressed the button for the ground floor, descending towards the reception lobby. The lobby was quiet, with only a few early risers milling about. Yolaine scanned the room, and that's when she saw him.

Pierce was standing by the reception desk, speaking to a woman. Yolaine froze in her tracks, her breath catching in her throat. The woman was strikingly beautiful. She was tall, appeared slim, had long, dark hair cascading down her back, and was dressed in a sophisticated outfit that suggested she was well-to-do. Yolaine's heart skipped a beat as she observed them.

The woman's face was grave, her brow furrowed, and Pierce seemed to be explaining something to her. Yolaine could see the tension in their body language — no warmth, no casual friendliness. Instead, their conversation was sharp, intense, and even heated. Pierce's hand gestures indicated his frustration, while the woman stood firm, her expression of disbelief or anger.

Yolaine felt a strange pang in her chest as she hid behind a nearby corridor wall, watching the exchange. She wasn't sure what to make of it. The argument wasn't just a casual disagreement; it seemed significant, as though something had deeply stirred them. Yolaine could hear the occasional raised voice, though the words were muffled and beyond her reach.

Yolaine's thoughts raced. *Who is she? What's going on here?* Her mind spun with questions. *Is Pierce involved with this woman?* What could they possibly be arguing about so early in the morning?

As the argument continued, Yolaine remained in the shadows, unable to take her eyes off the scene. The raw emotion and tension between them were palpable, and she couldn't help but wonder how this would affect everything. *What does this mean for me? For Pierce? For us?*

She stood momentarily longer, trying to understand what she had just witnessed, but the uncertainty gnawed at her. After a while, she saw Pierce grab the woman by the arms and guide her outside through the hotel's main exit. Yolaine's heart began to race as she followed them at a distance, her footsteps quiet on the hotel's polished floors.

The commotion between them continued as they moved outside. Pierce bent over, pulling the woman closer, and said something to her, his words muffled by the distance, leaving Yolaine unable to catch them. Her breath caught in her throat as she watched, her heart racing. Once tense and furious, the woman seemed to soften in response to Pierce's words. Her expression shifted subtly, the anger melting away, replaced by a calmer, more composed demeanour.

After a final, lingering look at Pierce, the woman turned, heading towards her car. She slipped inside, started the engine, and drove off with a sharp turn of the wheel, disappearing into the morning haze. Pierce remained standing, his eyes following her car as it vanished. His posture was rigid, and his hands rested on his hips as if trying to make sense of the whirlwind of emotions and events that had just unfolded. The weight of the moment hung heavily around him, the tension thick in the air as he stood there, alone with his thoughts.

Yolaine remained hidden in the shadows, her heart heavy with anger and confusion. *What just happened?* she wondered, the weight of the unknown pressing down on her, leaving her with more questions than answers. She turned and slowly returned to her room, each step heavier than the last. Once inside, she quietly crawled into bed beside Kaley, pretending to be asleep. Her mind was a whirlwind, but she needed Pierce to know she had seen everything.

It wasn't long before Pierce entered the room. He paused momentarily, noticing Yolaine lying beside Kaley, her breathing slow and steady, as if she had been asleep all along. He said nothing, but his gaze lingered on her momentarily before disappearing into the bathroom. Yolaine could hear the sound of running water, and the minutes seemed to stretch for eternity. Then, the distinct sound of the toilet flushing echoed through the room. Pierce emerged from the bathroom, his expression unreadable.

He moved toward the room phone, picking it up with purpose. He dialled the reception, calmly and collectedly informing them that they would check out early after breakfast. They were supposed to stay one more night, but plans had changed.

Yolaine didn't move. She stayed still, her eyes closed, pretending to sleep. On the other hand, Kaley stirred beside her, loudly yawning.

"Mama, you slept with me," she said, giggling as she stretched. "I thought I was with Dada!"

Yolaine didn't open her eyes. She lay there, her heart racing. Standing at the edge of the room, Pierce didn't speak either. The silence was thick with unspoken words, a tension neither seemed willing to break.

Finally, Yolaine shifted slightly, and Kaley sat up, rubbing her eyes. Pierce was already moving to freshen up, leaving the room in silence.

At breakfast, the atmosphere was strained. As if to break the tension, Pierce casually mentioned, "We'll have to cut the trip short. I've got an urgent business that needs my attention." His tone was even, though the words were sharp, as though he were speaking without emotion.

Kaley, looking disappointed, let out a dramatic sigh. "Ahhh, can't we stay longer?"

Pierce leaned in, trying to lighten the mood. "We'll come back soon, darling," he said, his voice softer as he tried to pacify her. "I promise. We'll have more fun next time." He made a playful noise, trying to make her giggle, but the effort seemed hollow, as if the weight of everything that had happened hung between them.

Yolaine didn't respond. Her silence was her answer, her mind too busy, too tangled in questions she wasn't sure she wanted the answers to. The air between them was thick and tense, but no one spoke of what had happened. The only sound in the restaurant dining hall was the clinking of cutlery and Kaley's reluctant laughter.

Yolaine had always doubted Pierce. Deep down, she knew there was something too perfect about him, something that didn't quite add up. In their early days of dating and throughout their marriage, there had been moments when she questioned his sincerity, but she pushed those thoughts away, convinced that he was too good to be true.

He had been different back then—more open, more present. There was a charm about him that she couldn't resist, a sophistication that seemed to shine through in every word he spoke. He spoke of grand dreams and ambitions that stretched far beyond the ordinary, and that was enough for a while. She was drawn to his strength, his determination to do something big, something that would set them apart from the rest. She had fallen for the idea of him just as much as for the man himself.

But as the years passed, Yolaine began to see the cracks. Pierce wasn't exactly the man she had hoped for, though she never expected to face the truth. When she was younger, she had never imagined that chasing dreams and ambition would come at such a steep price. But now, the reality was beginning to settle in.

His involvement with other women had worked because he knew how to charm them. It wasn't just his looks or words—how he made them feel special and could sweep them off their feet, just as he had done with her all those years ago. Yolaine had once been a willing prey to his charms, and now she could see the pattern. His allure was his weapon, and it had served him well.

The price of ambition, Yolaine realised, was not just about sacrificing time or comfort—it was about losing the person you once were and the trust of those closest to you.

She couldn't ignore it any longer. The man she had once fallen in love with had become a stranger, someone she was no longer sure she recognised. But she couldn't yet fully face the truth. The façade Pierce had built around himself was too convincing, and she wasn't ready to tear it down just yet. But the doubt lingered—*she knew* there was more to him than met the eye. And sooner or later, she would have to confront it.

After breakfast, they packed up and checked out of the hotel. The drive back was quiet, with Kaley happily chatting away in the backseat, her excitement over the trip still evident. Yolaine's mind, however, was elsewhere. It was clouded with uncertainty, and the nagging doubt had grown in her since she had witnessed Pierce's interaction with the woman. Pierce knew she was preoccupied, but he didn't ask her. He knew better than to bring it up. Asking her questions would only invite trouble for himself—there would be discussions, and he wasn't ready to answer them. So, he remained silent, the tension hanging between them like a heavy fog.

They pulled over during the journey to grab a drink and allow Kaley to use the washroom, stopping for a meal on their way home. The drive seemed endless, but eventually, they reached home in the afternoon.

Upon arrival, Yolaine quickly washed Kaley up and tucked her into bed for a nap. She stayed with her, lying beside her on the bed, holding Kaley close. The afternoon's quiet gave Yolaine some space to think, though her mind still circled back to the same troubling questions about Pierce.

She picked up her phone and messaged her brother, Edward. She needed an escape, some time away from everything, even for a little while.

*"I won't be able to join work on Monday,"* she wrote. *"I think I need a holiday."*

Edward quickly responded. *"Is everything okay?"* he asked. *"Today's only Saturday, so you have one more day to rest. You should be fine with returning on Monday; you'll have enough rest by then. I know you went off with Pierce and Kaley."*

Yolaine hesitated before responding, her fingers hovering over the keys. She didn't want to reveal everything but didn't want to lie.

*"I'm not feeling well. I may not be able to join back on Monday."*

Edward's reply was simple and understanding. *"Okay, take care."*

Yolaine put the phone down, but the weight of the conversation lingers. She glanced at Kaley, who was still peacefully asleep beside her, and hugged her tighter, trying to find comfort in her daughter's warmth. The room's quietness allowed her to rest, though her mind remained restless.

Meanwhile, Pierce was downstairs in the living room, absorbed in his phone. His usual energy seemed distant and subdued, possibly avoiding any real confrontation. He didn't acknowledge Yolaine's message or the heavy silence between them. It was easier that way—just a brief escape into the digital world, where he could hide from the tension at home.

That evening, the doorbell rang. Pierce opened the door to the delivery boy, paid him, and gave him a tip before bringing the food into the kitchen. He called out cheerfully, "Come on down, family! I've ordered your favourite meal!" His voice was light as if he hadn't just been avoiding the elephant in the room.

Already awake and excited, Kaley darted down the stairs, her little feet pattering on the floor. Yolaine followed more slowly, still feeling the weight of the day. They sat at the dining table; Kaley's face lit up when she saw the burgers and French fries before her. She happily dug into her meal, chattering about how much she loved the food.

Yolaine and Pierce sat quietly, eating their meals, the silence between them thick and uncomfortable. Neither of them spoke much, both lost in their thoughts. Once a source of comfort, the food seemed to have lost its warmth, as if the tension had seeped into everything around them.

Later that night, once Kaley had been put to bed, Yolaine retreated to her bedroom. Pierce was already there, sitting on the bed with a book. He didn't look up as she entered, and Yolaine didn't speak either. She changed into her nightclothes, her mind far from the book Pierce was absorbed in. She climbed into bed beside him, the space between them more distant than ever.

Pierce's eyes briefly flicked over to her, but he said nothing. He didn't want to bring up the awkwardness, just as Yolaine didn't. They both lay there in silence, each lost in their thoughts, the weight of their unsaid words pressing down on them.

Yolaine turned on her side, facing away from him. She couldn't shake the feeling that something had shifted permanently. Pierce was lying there next to her, yet he felt miles away. The tension between them had grown so thick that even sleep seemed out of reach.

She picked up her phone, her fingers hesitating for a moment before she typed a message to Aston. "Hi, how are you?" she sent, almost hoping for a distraction. Aston responded instantly as if eagerly waiting for her message.

"I'm fine. Where are you? There have been no calls or messages. I was a bit worried."

Yolaine paused before replying, trying to sound casual. "I'm fine, with family on vacation. Will see you soon when I'm back."

Aston's reply came quickly, "Miss you till then."

Yolaine smiled, the message offering a small comfort amidst her thoughts. She sent back a smiley emoji, hoping it conveyed the reassurance she didn't quite feel herself.

# #13
# Surrender to Desire

The morning light filtered through the curtains, casting a soft, golden glow across the room. Yolaine stirred from her sleep, the weight of the past few days still pressing heavily on her mind. She slowly rose from the bed, her movements slow and deliberate, before heading towards Kaley's bedroom. Gently, she woke her daughter, who was still yawning and drowsy.

Yolaine spoke to her in a sweet tone, "Come on, darling, let's get up and go out with Mama. We're going to church."

Kaley's eyes brightened, and she quickly shook off her drowsiness, excited at the thought. She jumped out of bed and began getting ready. They had a quick breakfast together, and then Yolaine drove them to Sunday mass, Kaley happily chattering beside her.

Meanwhile, Pierce remained in bed, still fast asleep.

Yolaine had always been a regular at church, finding comfort and peace in her prayers. But recently, her desire to go more often had grown, all because of Aston. He would be there, and she felt a strange pull to attend as if it might bring them closer.

At the church, Yolaine and Kaley made their way to the second row, the scent of incense mingling with the soft hum of voices around them. The atmosphere was familiar and comforting, but Yolaine couldn't shake the flutter of anticipation that stirred within her. As she glanced around the room, her eyes unexpectedly locked with Aston's. For a moment, everything else seemed to fade. Their gazes met with an almost imperceptible intensity—a quick, sharp glance followed by a knowing grin. It was as though the world had paused, just for that brief moment, and in that silent exchange, something unspoken passed between them.

As the mass ended, Aston made his way toward them. Yolaine stood as he approached, her heart beating a little faster, but she kept her composure, smoothing her dress and offering a polite smile. Aston, too, was trying to maintain his usual calm, but there was a noticeable nervous energy in how he carried himself. Despite the formal greetings, it was as if something more was bubbling just beneath the surface.

"Good to see you," Aston said, his voice steady but betraying the emotions he was trying to keep in check.

Yolaine nodded, keeping things formal. "It's good to see you too, Aston."

He hesitated as if there was more he wanted to say, but time was pressing on. He had other responsibilities and people to attend to, and his commitments to the brotherhood weighed on him. "I have to go," he said reluctantly, his voice tinged with regret. "I've got other things to take care of."

Yolaine watched him walk away, her thoughts momentarily lost in her pull toward him. Aston had always struck her as genuine—a sweet, down-to-earth man with a heart of gold—unlike the type of men she usually encountered, like Pierce. Her thoughts were interrupted as Kaley tugged at her hand, her excitement to head home breaking the spell.

The drive back was quiet. Kaley chattered about everything and nothing, but Yolaine's mind was elsewhere. She couldn't help but think of Aston, his kind eyes and unassuming nature, and how he made her feel at ease. She pushed those thoughts aside, though, not wanting to dwell on them, knowing they weren't something she could effortlessly chase after. Not yet, anyway.

When they arrived home, they were greeted by an unexpected sight—Pierce had prepared a meal for them. It was a surprise, to say the least. Yolaine raised an eyebrow as she stepped through the door. "Lunch is ready," Pierce said, his voice casual but with a certain edge.

Kaley's face lit up. "Dada, dada!" she exclaimed, running toward her father.

Yolaine couldn't help but smile slightly. "That's new," she muttered under her breath. Pierce wasn't one to cook unless he tried to distract or prove something. It was an odd gesture, but Yolaine didn't comment further. She just nodded, surprised yet unsure of what to make of it.

They sat down at the table, and despite the simplicity of the meal, there was a warmth in the gesture. The conversation was light, Kaley eagerly talking about her day, her favourite cartoons, and everything that caught her attention. Pierce was more absorbed in his phone than in the family moment. Yolaine watched him quietly, her smile polite but distant. She couldn't help but feel that something was off, something that lingered beneath the surface.

After the meal, they all moved to the living room. Kaley plopped down in front of the TV, eagerly settling in for her favourite cartoon show. Yolaine kept herself calm, watching her daughter with a soft smile, but her thoughts drifted back to the conversation she'd been holding with herself all day. Pierce had been so distant recently, his behaviour odd, and that woman at the hotel lobby—Yolaine couldn't shake the feeling that something was off.

The silence between them stretched on, thick with unspoken thoughts. Finally, breaking it, Yolaine spoke. Her voice was unnervingly calm, almost too rehearsed. "Who was that lady who came to meet you in the hotel lobby this morning?" Her eyes remained locked on Kaley, but her mind focused entirely on Pierce.

Pierce didn't respond right away. His fingers hovered over his phone, eyes flicking between the screen and Yolaine. His expression stayed unreadable as if he was weighing his words carefully. After a beat, he finally spoke, his tone casual, betraying nothing. "She's the wife of my business partner. She had some issues with him and needed my help. That's why she came all the way to meet me. I helped her sort things out. That's all."

Yolaine's eyes shifted from Kaley to Pierce, narrowing slightly. She studied him, then asked, her voice sharp but controlled, "How did she know where to find us?"

For the first time, Pierce's gaze flicked away from her. His fingers twitched on his phone, but he didn't answer immediately. When he did, his voice was calm, almost too quiet. "I informed her," he said, the words coming out in a measured tone. "I didn't know what else to do. My partner asked me to help out."

Yolaine wasn't convinced. Something about how he said it—the rehearsed calmness, the way he avoided her gaze—made her uneasy. She knew Pierce better than that. He was hiding something, and she could feel it. But instead of pushing him further, she nodded. Over the years, she had learned that questioning him too much would only lead to more lies. So, she let it slide—for now.

The day passed without incident, and soon it was evening. Pierce got up, telling her he had an important meeting with his partners. "I'll be back soon," he said, and Yolaine gave him a quiet nod. No words of protest, no arguments. She didn't need to ask where he was going or what he was doing. She had learned not to push.

That night, Pierce returned late. Yolaine was already in bed, pretending to sleep, her mind racing. She heard him move about the room, the soft rustle of his clothes as he freshened up, and the creak of the bed as he settled beside her. A strange stillness in the air, a distance that had grown between them. He didn't disturb her. He respected the space between them as if he knew silence was safer than confronting whatever was left unsaid.

Yolaine lay still, her eyes open in the darkness. She could hear his steady breathing beside her. Her thoughts, however, were far from peaceful. Aston, the lady at the hotel, felt Pierce's strange behaviour swirl in her mind, yet she kept it all inside. She didn't speak. She didn't ask. There was no point. It was safer this way.

As the night stretched on, Yolaine finally drifted off to sleep. The tension between her and Pierce was thick, but neither spoke. Neither made a move to change the silence. It was as if they both understood that sometimes, silence was the only thing that could hold everything together.

The following morning, the beginning of the week arrived with the usual routine. It was time for Kaley to get ready for school, and as always, Yolaine was up early, preparing for the busy day ahead. The house was still quiet, save for the soft rustle of the morning breeze through the curtains. Yolaine moved around the kitchen, getting things for breakfast. Her mind was a mixture of thoughts—some mundane, others much more unsettling.

As usual, the maid arrived early, and the woman was hired to support Yolaine during the week. She was there to help with everything—from cleaning to organising- but always respected Yolaine's preferences. The maid was someone Yolaine relied on, yet she respected their arrangement: the maid would leave on weekends, as Yolaine preferred to handle things herself during that time. The maid, too, enjoyed spending her weekends with her family, but she was always available if Yolaine needed assistance.

Yolaine moved through the house, her footsteps soft but purposeful, and headed straight for Kaley's room. She knocked gently before stepping inside. Kaley was already stirring, stretching and blinking sleepily as the morning light filled the room. Yolaine smiled warmly at her daughter's sleepy face, the smile of quiet affection. "Good morning, sweetheart," she whispered, moving to help her prepare.

With practised hands, Yolaine guided Kaley into her school uniform, which had been carefully laid out the night before. The little rituals of their life together were comforting in their predictability. Kaley was excited, chatting about her day ahead as Yolaine helped with her hair, braiding it neatly. It felt like any other day, but beneath the surface, Yolaine couldn't shake the feeling that things were far from normal.

As she helped Kaley gather her things, her thoughts wandered. The house was unnervingly quiet. Pierce had already left for work—early as usual. She knew why. The brief exchange they'd had the previous evening still lingered, unfinished and hanging between them. He had left early this morning, likely hoping Yolaine wouldn't press him for more answers. She knew him too well. He was trying to avoid another confrontation.

She couldn't blame him for trying but couldn't let it go. She had so many questions and things left unsaid, and Pierce knew it. Yet, there was a sense of powerlessness that weighed heavily on Yolaine. Something held her back despite her desire to confront him and demand the truth. Maybe it was the routine of their life, or perhaps the fear that the truth would be something she didn't want to hear. Either way, the conversation would happen—she was sure of it.

Once Kaley was ready, the mother and daughter stood by the door together. Yolaine's heart swelled as she watched Kaley eagerly run out the door onto the bus, which always stopped outside their lawn. It was a simple routine that gave the day a sense of normalcy. Yolaine stood there momentarily, watching the bus pull away, feeling the world's weight pressing down her shoulders.

She took a deep breath, trying to calm herself. *Enough of this,* she thought. She had carried this burden for far too long. The unresolved tension with Pierce, the questions, and the distance started pulling her under. She knew it was time to focus on herself. No more letting things slide, no more holding her tongue. She needed to take control and regain some semblance of peace in her own life.

With that thought, Yolaine closed the door behind her and returned to face the day. The morning had started as any other, but for the first time in a while, Yolaine felt the stirrings of something new—a resolve, a determination. It was time to address the things simmering beneath the surface. She couldn't keep living like this.

Reaching for her phone, Yolaine dialled Aston's number, her fingers lingering on the screen momentarily before pressing send. The phone rang twice before he answered.

"Yolaine," Aston's voice was warm and inviting. "How are you?"

"I need to see you," Yolaine said, her voice laced with an urgency she hadn't anticipated. "Can we meet up? I just… I need a change of scenery, and I think you might help me clear my head."

Aston's voice softened, sensing the tension in her words. "Of course. I'll be ready. Where do you want to meet?"

Yolaine quickly agreed on a time and place. After she hung up, she moved through the house in a daze, gathering her thoughts. She felt something deep inside stir—a need to reclaim her life and desires. She bathed, the hot water soothing her body and washing away the frustrations building for so long. As the water enveloped her, she let herself sink into the warmth, imagining the release she was about to embrace.

When she stepped out of the bath, she dressed in a way that felt different from the woman she had been the past few days. She chose a dress that clung to her curves, not for anyone else, but for herself. It was an act of reclaiming her power and reminding herself that she was more than the hurt, the betrayal, and the silence.

The drive to meet Aston was silent, but within Yolaine, a storm was brewing. She wasn't entirely sure what she was searching for, but something deep within her told her she might find it in his presence. The closer she got, the more palpable the tension became. When she arrived, Aston was already waiting, leaning casually against his car, expressing quiet anticipation. As soon as their eyes met, that connection they had been trying to ignore flared up—an undeniable spark simmering for weeks.

Without a word, Yolaine stepped forward. Aston's hand reached out for hers, and the instant their skin touched, a rush of heat shot up her arm, sending a jolt through her entire being. She couldn't define what this was, nor could she predict how it would unfold, but she knew, deep down, she needed this. There was no need for words; the silence between them was filled with a mutual understanding, a silent agreement of what they both craved.

Aston opened the car door for her, his movements smooth and steady, almost as though he had been waiting for this moment for as long as she had. They set off, and the road seemed endless, stretching out before them like a ribbon, but with each passing mile, Yolaine could feel the tension in her body loosen. The world outside faded, slipping away until the two of them were driving aimlessly into the unknown. At this moment, it wasn't about the destination—it was about the feeling of his presence beside her, the comfort in the closeness.

The drive seemed to go on forever. Each mile stretched the tension, thickening the air between them. Glances were exchanged—brief, charged with unspoken words—but no words passed between them. Aston knew precisely what was coming next. He was patient, waiting for her to decide what she wanted. Yolaine could feel the warmth radiating from him, a quiet, simmering hunger that grew with each passing second. She couldn't ignore the pull that had been building between them for so long. Every glance at him, every subtle shift of his body, made her pulse quicken.

She saw the same longing reflected in his eyes, and it only intensified the hunger she felt within herself. The atmosphere between them was electric, thick with anticipation, and the tension was almost unbearable. She knew they were both on the edge of something, and the only way forward was to give in.

When the car finally came to a stop, somewhere on the edge of a barren stretch of road, the outside world seemed to vanish. The only sounds were the car's engine's soft hum, the wind's quiet rush, and the steady thrum of their hearts, beating faster in unison. Aston turned to face her, his dark and intense gaze shivering through her. Without a word, he reached for her, his hand gently cupping her face, his thumb brushing over her jaw in a tender movement that took her breath away. At that moment, everything else ceased to exist—it was just the two of them and the promise of something they both knew they couldn't walk away from.

Yolaine leaned into his touch, her pulse racing as he pulled her closer. Their lips met softly at first, tentative, as though they were both testing the waters of their desire. The kiss was slow, almost agonisingly gentle, as if they had all the time in the world to savour each moment, each touch. But it didn't take long for the kiss to deepen, to grow more urgent. Yolaine felt her body respond, her hands instinctively reaching for his chest, feeling the warmth of his body beneath the fabric of his shirt. She pressed closer, the need to be near him overwhelming.

Aston groaned softly, his hand sliding down her back, pulling her tighter against him. The kiss deepened, becoming more demanding, more desperate. His lips parted, his tongue tracing the line of her lips before slipping inside, tasting her. Yolaine's breath caught in her throat, her body trembling under his touch as the kiss grew fiercer. The connection between them was undeniable, and she felt it intensifying, slowly consuming her. Every inch of her skin seemed to respond to his touch, her body pressing closer, wanting more.

His hands slid lower, moving over the curve of her waist. Yolaine shivered as he caressed her, his touch slow and deliberate, as though he was savouring every inch of her. The way his hands moved over her body made her feel alive, every nerve in her body humming with anticipation. His lips left hers, trailing kisses down her neck, his breath warm against her skin. She tilted her head back, offering more of herself to him, and she moaned softly as his lips moved lower, grazing her collarbone, each kiss sending a wave of pleasure through her.

Aston's hands continued their journey down her body, moving slowly as if he wanted to explore every curve, every line. He reached the hem of her dress, and with a deliberate slowness, he slid it upward. The soft fabric glided over her skin, and Yolaine felt the cool air kiss her exposed flesh. She shivered, not from the cold but from the heat of his touch. Her heart raced as the dress inched higher, revealing more of her, until it finally fell away, leaving her completely bare before him.

Aston gazed at her for a long moment, his eyes dark with desire, taking in every inch of her exposed skin. There was no shame, only raw, unspoken longing. His gaze was filled with admiration, and she felt a rush of warmth flood her body. She wanted him—needed him—more than she could express in words.

Without breaking their gaze, Aston's hands moved to her chest, gently cupping her breasts. The touch was slow and deliberate, and when his thumbs brushed over her hardened nipples, Yolaine gasped, the sensation sending a jolt of pleasure through her. She arched into him, her body responding to him instinctively, the heat between them growing with every passing second. His fingers explored her softly, teasing her, and she felt a shiver of anticipation crawl down her spine.

"Oh, Aston, I've missed this...." Aston complied.

Aston's lips travelled to her breasts, kissing, tasting, and caressing her in a way that made her entire body shiver. He took his time, savouring each moment, every inch of her skin. Aston knew how beautiful Yolaine was—he recognised that she was a once-in-a-lifetime experience for him. The softness of her skin, the gentle curve of her neck, the way her eyes sparkled with a quiet strength—everything about her captivated him. Her delicate features, her hair fell in waves around her shoulders, and the smoothness of her body felt like a masterpiece in his hands. She was a perfect balance of grace and intensity, and he couldn't help but lose himself in her.

Yolaine moaned softly, her body arching into him, craving more. The intensity between them grew, and she felt herself becoming lost in the sensation of him, the taste of his lips, the feel of his hands on her.

"I want more," Yolaine whispered, her voice thick with need, eyes locked on his. Aston didn't speak—his hands slid down her body, strong fingers brushing the curve of her hips, then dipping to the edge of her panties. He moved slowly, teasing, peeling them down her thighs inch by inch. Yolaine's breath hitched, her chest rising fast as the heat of his touch burned through her. She shut her eyes, lost in the feel of his hands, the way they sparked shivers across her skin.

When the fabric fell away, she stood bare before him, heart pounding, bold yet fragile. Aston's gaze devoured her, dark with love and hunger. He pulled her close, kissing her hard, lips crashing with a fierce need. His fingers traced her inner thighs, soft but deliberate, inching toward her core. Each touch sent jolts through her, her body aching for him. She pressed against him, feeling his hard length throb against her folds. He thrust deeper, slow and intense, and she gasped, urging him on with every shift of her hips.

Their bodies fit like they were made for this—her straddling him, his hands gripping her tight. She slid onto him, wet and ready, his heat filling her as he pushed up to meet her. Their rhythm was perfect, urgent, a dance of love and fire. She kissed him deep, tongues tangling, the slow grind of their hips igniting her insides. His hands roamed to her bottom, squeezing firm, pulling her down harder as he thrust, each move building the storm between them.

The pressure grew wild and unstoppable. Every thrust rocked her, her breaths turning to moans. Aston's grip tightened, guiding her faster, their bodies slick with sweat. "I'm close," he rasped, voice rough with want. "Don't stop," she begged, pressing her chest to his, her thighs trembling as they chased the edge together. The air crackled with their need, every touch a promise.

Then it broke. Yolaine shook, a cry tearing free as her folds pulsed, his heat flooding her. Aston groaned deep, jerking hard as he spilled inside, his arms crushing her to him. They clung there, breathless, hearts slamming in sync. Her lips brushed his jaw; his breath warmed her neck. The world faded—just them, wrapped in love, fierce and tender. She met his gaze—eyes soft, endless. No words. Only them, bound tight in the glow.

Yolaine rested her head against Aston's chest, listening to the steady rhythm of his heartbeat beneath her ear. Her body still hummed with the intensity of their connection, and a sense of peace settled over her. At that moment, the hunger and longing had been fulfilled, and something deeper had been found—an understanding, a quiet contentment that neither had expected.

"Thank you, Aston," she whispered, kissing his chest softly.

Aston's hand gently stroked her hair. "No," he replied softly. "I should be thanking you. You're incredible."

Yolaine slid back into the driver's seat, her fingers brushing her hair as she adjusted it with a practised motion. She took a moment to breathe deeply, steadying herself. On the other hand, Aston picked up his trousers, zipping them up with a quiet focus, before tucking in his shirt. The car filled with a comfortable silence, neither of them speaking, yet the air between them felt heavy with something unspoken.

After a long moment, Yolaine's gaze shifted towards Aston. She reached out, her fingers gently tracing his jawline. It was a delicate touch, almost as if memorising his feel. Aston's eyes softened, and without hesitation, he kissed her hands, his lips lingering on her skin for just a second longer than necessary. He met her gaze, holding it as if nothing else mattered. His smile was small, yet full of quiet understanding, his eyes never leaving hers.

Without a word, Yolaine turned the key in the ignition and slowly drove off, the quiet hum of the car filling the space. She drove silently, lost in thought until they reached the church compound. She parked, her hands gripping the steering wheel for a moment before she finally spoke, though her words seemed distant as if meant for herself. "I'll see you soon," she murmured, not looking back.

Aston didn't answer immediately, but his eyes followed her as she drove off, leaving him alone outside the gates.

Yolaine returned home shortly after. The moment she stepped out of the car, the servant greeted her at the door, eyes widening slightly. It was clear something was different; Yolaine's usual composed appearance was slightly dishevelled—her hair was not as neat, and her expression was more distant than when she left. The servant hesitated momentarily but said nothing, merely stepping aside to let her pass.

Yolaine gave a slight nod and walked past him, her mind elsewhere. She headed upstairs, the soft click of her shoes echoing in the quiet hallway. Once inside her room, she quickly undressed and headed for a quick bath, trying to shake off the emotions that still clung to her. She needed to clear her mind, especially with Kaley returning from school any moment now. The tension in her body refused to loosen, and she took a long, deep breath, hoping the water would wash away the weight she carried.

That evening, Pierce couldn't help but notice a shift in Yolaine. She seemed different—far more calm and composed than usual. She was playing with Kaley, her laughter ringing out, a smile gracing her face that Pierce hadn't seen in some time. It was a warmth that seemed unfamiliar, almost foreign, leaving him momentarily unsettled. He watched her from across the room;

his brow furrowed as he tried to make sense of the sudden change. It was as though a weight had been lifted from her shoulders, but he couldn't quite place what had caused it.

Later that night, as they lay in bed, Pierce moved closer to Yolaine, his hand reaching out to gently touch her arm. There was a familiar tension between them, which had existed in the past but now felt more pronounced. It was an unspoken understanding that they both recognised but neither addressed.

However, Yolaine didn't respond to his advances. Instead, she turned away, her back facing him, her body stiff with a quiet resistance. Pierce's hand hung in the air momentarily before falling to his side. His eyes lingered on her for a second, a mixture of frustration and confusion bubbling inside him, before he sighed softly and lay back against the pillows.

Yolaine, on the other hand, seemed entirely at ease. Her breathing evened out, a peaceful calmness settling over her as she drifted into a deep sleep, her back still turned to him.

Before closing her eyes, Yolaine reached for her phone on the bedside table, her fingers moving with practised grace. She sent a simple, deliberate message: *Good night, Aston.*

A few moments passed before her phone buzzed with his reply: *Good night, Yolaine. Do you want to meet again tomorrow?*

She hesitated briefly, her fingers hovering over the screen, before typing her response: *Let you know tomorrow, darling.*

The words hung in the quiet air of the room, and though Pierce hadn't seen the message, he felt the silent weight between them. Something unspoken, a quiet distance that neither had addressed but both could feel.

Yolaine put the phone down, her eyes closing slowly, her face serene as the night drew close. She left Pierce awake in the stillness; their gap seemed more expansive than ever.

# #14
# Heart's Call

As soon as Kaley left for school, Yolaine didn't waste a second. She moved swiftly, gathering her things with purpose, her mind already set on what needed to be done. Her gaze flicked briefly toward Pierce, still lounging around the house, unaware of her plans. She didn't care what he thought. There was no need to inform him; she had no intention of explaining herself. Her movements were sharp, deliberate—like a silent declaration of independence. She was done waiting, trying to make sense of the chaos between them.

She pulled out her phone and messaged Edward, her brother. She would need to take an additional leave and couldn't make it to work. Edward knew something was wrong, but he also knew Yolaine well enough to trust that she could handle her situation. His reply was simple: *"Fine. Take care."*

Yolaine didn't need more than that. She dressed in something effortlessly stylish—an outfit that made her feel confident and free. It wasn't just the clothing; it was the armour she needed, the final touch to remind herself that she was in control of her decisions. Her heels clicked against the floor as she grabbed her keys, each step more resolute than the last.

She stole one last glance at Pierce as she walked out the door. He was still unaware, still absorbed in his world. The weight of the past lingered between them, but it no longer felt like a burden she had to carry. With one final breath, Yolaine stepped outside, the door closing behind her. The moment was hers, and she felt truly free for the first time in a long while.

Yolaine was determined to take control of her day. She had already messaged Aston, telling him to meet her, and now there was no turning back. She slid into her car, the engine purring to life beneath her, and drove off.

The drive was a release. The wind in her hair and the hum of the road beneath her tyres felt like she was breaking free from the invisible chains holding her down. She had a need, a desire to feel alive, to feel seen, and right now, that meant being with someone who gave her the attention she craved. Pierce had failed to provide that for her lately. He was distant, too wrapped up in his world. Aston, however, was different. He looked at her like she was the only one in the room as if she mattered.

She reached the church compound, and he was there waiting for her. Aston's eyes locked onto hers when she pulled up, a smile tugging at his lips. Without a word, he slid into the car, and she didn't waste any time before accelerating, driving them both away from the familiar and heading towards the unknown.

Their conversation flowed easily, but the air was thick with unspoken tension. Yolaine wasn't sure whether it was how Aston looked at her or how he leaned in just a little too close whenever he spoke, but she felt the pull between them, undeniable. She wasn't thinking about consequences or what Pierce might say—this was for her. The chemistry between her and Aston was electric, starkly contrasting the coldness she'd been feeling at home.

The car was quiet momentarily as they sped down the road, but Aston's hand found hers, his fingers grazing the side of her palm. The touch was soft yet charged with an intensity that sent a rush of heat through her body. Yolaine's breath hitched, and she looked over at him, eyes meeting his with a mixture of desire and defiance. The freedom in the air, the drive rush—it was intoxicating.

Aston's hand slid up her arm, his touch now more assertive, his fingertips grazing the bare skin of her neck. She didn't pull away. Instead, she leaned into the touch, her pulse quickening as they drove further, the world outside disappearing. The car became a cocoon, a private world where the only thing that mattered was how he made her feel. Every glance, every touch seemed to unravel something inside her that had been hidden for too long. She wasn't just seeking attention anymore; she was seeking affirmation, validation that she was worthy of something more.

They didn't speak much, but the silence between them was heavy with anticipation. As they found an isolated spot, away from prying eyes, Yolaine finally allowed herself to give in to the moment. She kissed him, a kiss full of urgency, as if she had been holding her breath for far too long. Aston responded with the same intensity, his hands on her, guiding her, pulling her closer. The world outside faded entirely as they lost themselves in each other.

For a long time, it was just the two of them, the intensity of their connection building with every passing second. When it was over, Yolaine sat back in her seat, breathing heavily, her heart pounding. She had gotten what she needed. In this moment, she felt seen, wanted, and more alive than she had in what felt like forever.

With the air between them a little quieter, she turned the car around and drove him back. The silence was comfortable, though there was a weight to it, an unspoken understanding. She dropped him off with a casual goodbye, and he watched as she drove off without a word.

When she returned home, to her surprise, Pierce was still there. He was in the study, focused on his work. Yolaine stepped inside, her mind still reeling from the intensity of her time with Aston. She didn't care to explain herself; she moved past him, her steps steady, betraying none of the turmoil inside.

She headed straight for the bathroom, the cool water soothing her heated skin. The steam from the shower fogged up the mirrors, but it did little to wash away the lingering feelings of the day. She wanted to forget what had just happened, but she couldn't. A part of her felt a little lighter and more empowered, but another part felt hollow like something had been left behind.

Kaley returned from school, and the servant opened the door to let her in. The child was ushered inside and cleaned up, and Yolaine took over, as usual, feeding her and tending to her needs. The house, however, felt oddly quiet. The usual routine resumed, but beneath it all, the emotional storm Yolaine had just gone through seemed to hang in the air, unspoken. Pierce stayed in the study, his eyes occasionally flicking to Yolaine, but he said nothing.

He was watching her. Yolaine could feel his gaze, though she didn't acknowledge it. Her mind was elsewhere, and for the first time in a long time, she didn't care what Pierce thought.

Pierce was sharp and perceptive. Over the years, he'd learned to read Yolaine better than anyone else could. He knew when she made a decision, nothing could change her mind. She was determined and focused, and it was almost impossible to steer her off course once she set her intentions. He noticed the subtle but unmistakable shifts in her recently—how her smiles sometimes seemed forced, how her eyes lingered on him in a way that suggested she wasn't *there*. Her heart, he realised, was no longer with him.

For the next few days, Pierce kept an eye on her. She'd leave the house at strange times, not saying where she was going, and when she came back, there was a coldness about her as she had been somewhere far away. There was a shift in her energy—she seemed a little reckless as if she was living on her terms and doing whatever felt right. Pierce hadn't seen this side of her before.

She was pulling away, and it felt like she was trying to find something—

maybe herself, maybe something she had lost. Pierce noticed that when they were together, she wasn't entirely there. Her attention was scattered, and the warmth she once had when she looked at him was gone. He couldn't help but wonder how long she would keep up this behaviour or what she was looking for.

Instead of confronting her, Pierce stayed quiet, watching from a distance. The changes in her only piqued his curiosity. Was she acting out because of what had happened at the hotel? Was she trying to fill a void he couldn't? Pierce wasn't sure, but he knew pressing her would only push her further away. Yolaine was proud and wouldn't take kindly to being forced into a conversation she wasn't ready for.

He decided to wait, observing quietly. Pierce knew something was driving her, but he couldn't figure it out. The memory of the hotel incident still stung, and he had seen the hurt in her eyes, even though she tried to hide it. Yolaine wasn't the type to confront him directly, so instead, she was keeping him at a distance, taking control of her life in small, subtle ways.

#15

# The Calm Before the Storm

Yolaine eventually realised that she was getting carried away. She couldn't afford to lose herself to get back at Pierce. Kaley was her priority, and the child had been neglected amid everything happening. This didn't sit well with Yolaine—it wasn't the woman she had worked so hard to become, the one who valued stability and maintaining balance for the sake of her family. The reckless behaviour she had been indulging in didn't align with who she was. She needed to regroup, get back to her routine, and retake control of her life.

As she began to settle, Yolaine noticed that Pierce had been calm and composed. He had given her space, refraining from pushing her into confrontations or trying to intimidate her. There had been no heated arguments, and for the first time in a while, she recognised the peace he was trying to maintain in their home. That shift in his behaviour helped her cool off, and she felt a sense of calm returning.

Pierce, for his part, maintained his composure. While Yolaine navigated her emotional upheaval, he focused on caring for Kaley. He ensured the house ran smoothly, maintaining a sense of stability for their family. He knew things were fragile and didn't want to escalate the situation. He also knew he was partly responsible for their tension and didn't want to lose her. He hoped that, with time, things could be repaired.

As the days passed, Yolaine gradually returned to her usual routine. She continued to contact Aston, and their casual chats and flirtations picked up where they had left off. She usually went to church, which was always formal whenever they met. Aston didn't push her; he was content to do whatever she wanted. He knew she was married and had a life to navigate, but he would be ready if she ever decided to leave everything behind.

Over time, Yolaine and Pierce began speaking again. Their conversations were cautious at first, but they slowly started to return to a more familiar pattern. Pierce decided it was time to throw himself back into his work. There were pressing matters that required his attention, so he was scheduled to go on a business trip. This time, he would be away for more than two weeks.

The night before Pierce's flight, the family had a quiet dinner together, sitting in the soft glow of the dining room light. After the meal, they watched some television, and the atmosphere was peaceful, if not strained. Kaley, exhausted from the day, yawned and curled up beside them. Pierce smiled warmly, lifting her into his arms.

"I'll put her to bed," he said gently, heading upstairs to her room. Yolaine watched him, her eyes following them as they disappeared up the stairs. She knew he was a good father—there was no doubt about that. But her thoughts always went back to the man who had let her down, the man who had failed to be the husband she needed. The tenderness he showed Kaley only made the distance between them feel more profound. The love they once shared felt so far away now, and it hurt.

Yolaine knew she had made choices she wasn't proud of. Her need for comfort and attention had led her to seek it elsewhere. And while Pierce was putting Kaley to bed, she couldn't help but feel a heavy guilt weighing on her. She needed space to clear her head and escape the emotional mess she'd been living in.

She left the room quietly, heading for the bath. The warm water wrapped around her like a temporary escape, allowing her to relax as the steam filled the room. But no matter how hard she tried, the thoughts of everything that had happened kept creeping back into her mind.

When she was done and fresh from the bath, Pierce had already returned to the bedroom. He was sitting on the edge of the bed, his phone in his hand.

"She's asleep," he said, his voice casual as he glanced up at her. "I'm going for a quick shower."

Yolaine nodded but said nothing, watching as he disappeared into the bathroom. She took her time changing into a soft nightdress, the familiar motions grounding her as she applied lotion and cream. The scent of lavender filled the air, offering a brief moment of comfort.

When Pierce returned, his damp hair falling slightly over his forehead, he dried himself off and climbed into bed beside her. The room was dimly lit, just enough to give it a soft, romantic glow, though the tension between them lingered, unsaid and unresolved. Yolaine reached over and dimmed the lights further, the room now bathed in a soft, intimate light.

Neither of them spoke. Pierce lay on his side, his back turned slightly toward her, though his eyes were open, reflecting the tension between them. Yolaine remained still, unsure of what to say or do. The space between them felt vast, yet there was a strange comfort in the silence.

The air was thick with unspoken words. Yolaine's mind raced, torn between the desire for closeness and the frustration that had been building. Pierce lay beside her, his presence comforting, but the absence of the warmth they once shared filled the space. She could feel its weight, but neither moved to change it.

Pierce moved closer to Yolaine with a slow, unhurried rhythm, each motion measured as though he wanted the moment to stretch, to last longer between them. His body hovered just inches from hers, and when he was so close that she could feel his breath, the air between them thickened with tension. Yolaine didn't move, but inside, a swirl of emotions stirred within her, emotions she hadn't let herself feel in a long time. She wanted him. She longed for him, for the closeness they had once shared. He was still the man she had married—the father of their child. That connection was undeniable, no matter what had happened.

Pierce's hand brushed lightly against hers, a tentative touch at first. She didn't pull away; her fingers tightened around him as if she had been waiting. Slowly, he brought her hand to his lips, pressing a gentle kiss to her knuckles before holding it against his chest, the warmth of his touch grounding her. She held onto him, matching the intensity of his grip, the tension between them palpable.

His hand moved down her arm, his fingers tracing a path over her skin, lingering for a moment before gently pulling at the strap of her nightdress. It slid down easily, exposing the soft curve of her shoulder. Yolaine's breath caught in her throat, her heart racing, but she didn't stop him. Instead, she leaned into his touch, her body responding in a way she hadn't allowed in months.

Pierce's lips followed the path of his fingers, brushing over her shoulder and neck. His kisses were slow, almost reverent, as though rediscovering her, cherishing every inch of her skin. Yolaine's breath grew shallow, her pulse quickening. She could feel her body responding to him, the familiar pull of desire surging within her. Pierce kissed the curve of her neck, then moved slowly down to her collarbone.

She closed her eyes, surrendering to the sensation, letting herself feel every moment. There was no rush. Just the weight of his presence beside her, the soft, rhythmic press of his lips against her skin, and the gentle way he held her. His hand moved to the other strap of her nightdress, slowly, deliberately easing it down until it fell away, revealing her skin to him in the soft glow of the room.

Pierce paused, his gaze lingering on her, full of admiration and longing. He hadn't realised how much he had missed this—how much he had missed her.

Yolaine's breath grew heavier, and the warmth of the room and the heat building between them made it hard to think straight. She didn't stop him; instead, she reached for him, pulling him closer, her fingers threading through his hair, urging him on. Pierce's lips moved to her chest, the slow, tender kisses now moving with more urgency as he traced every curve with his mouth.

Her heart raced, the pulse of longing surging through her as Pierce's lips found the soft yet firm curve of her breast. Yolaine gasped, her body arching instinctively towards him, unable to resist the magnetic pull between them. Pierce's hands were gentle yet firm as he caressed her body with careful attention, moving from her hips upward to her chest. His fingers brushed her skin once more, sending a shiver through her. Slowly, his hand moved to her breast, teasing with a soft pinch to the nipple while his lips gently teased the other. The sensation made her gasp, her body arching instinctively, her breath quickening as she responded to his touch.

Yolaine's body stirred with longing, her fingers sinking into Pierce's back, pulling him near as their old love flickered back, fierce and untamed. Her walls faded, and she surrendered—raw, open, trembling with lust and trust. Pierce eased her nightdress down, his fingers lingering on her skin with a gentleness that set her quivering. She arched into him, letting the fabric slip away, her breasts bared, nipples hardening in the cool air under his smouldering gaze.

She wasn't wearing anything underneath, almost like she had prepared herself for this moment, both in mind and body. The room's chill brushed her skin, but his eyes—blazing with reverence, longing, and deep hunger—warmed her, her heart thumping wild in her chest.

Fear dissolved—only a sharp, aching need pulsed through her. His stare laid her bare, and she felt cherished, craved, as their lips met—soft, then urgent, a promise heavy with heat. Pierce drew her close, hands steady and possessive, tracing her curves with a tender, ravenous touch. Her breasts pressed against his chest, hard nipples grazing him, sparking a slow burn deep inside her—no rush—just the fierce urge to melt into him, like she'd always wanted.

Their kiss deepened, breaths uneven, the air thick with their quiet fire. Every touch wove them tighter, heart and soul. Pierce eased her leg over his hip, their bodies fitting snugly, no distance left. His hand drifted from her waist to her bottom, squeezing gently, fingers pressing in before sliding to her thighs, teasing near her core with a slow, worshipping stroke that made her pulse hum.

Yolaine's breath caught, her body shivering with want as his touch kindled a molten bond. The tension built, steady and electric, a heat they couldn't resist. Pierce lowered her to the bed, and she opened for him—bold, vulnerable, his. He shed his shorts, his length hard and ready, yearning for her in the soft light. He cradled her legs, parting them with a lover's care, then leaned in, kissing her inner thighs inch by inch—soft, reverent—before rising to meet her eyes, dark with a hunger that echoed hers. His length promised to claim her entirely, and she ached for it, for him to take her slow and deep.

He pressed closer, his body folding over hers, and she welcomed him—open, eager. As his length eased into her, stretching her folds, she sighed, a soft cry slipping free, her nipples peaking against him. The intensity simmered, drawing her into their union. Their rhythm unfolded gently, hips rocking in a slow dance, her breasts trembling with each careful thrust, hard nipples brushing his skin, sending shivers through her.

He took his time, deliberate—each stroke long and languid, his length savouring her, exploring her inch by inch. His mouth left hers, trailing warm kisses down her neck, across her collarbone, and then settling on her breast. He sucked her nipples slowly, teasing them with his tongue just as she loved, matching the unhurried thrusts. "Goodness, you're bloody stunning," he murmured against her skin, voice thick with awe. "Missed this—missed you, love." Yolaine moaned softly, her bottom lifting to meet him. "Keep going, Pierce—I need you," she whispered, voice laced with longing, their love a living pulse between them.

"I'm close," he breathed, raw and hushed, teetering on the edge. "In or out?" "In," she pleaded, her voice trembling, her breasts rising as he thrust deeper, slow and sure. He groaned, low and ragged, and he cum into her—hot, endless—flooding her, her core tightening around him.

"Love you, Yolaine," he whispered as he spilt, and she clung to him, breathless, hearts beating as one.

"I love you too," she sighed, her lips brushing his jaw, his breath weaving into her hair. It was fierce and tender, theirs—love and lust so deep it bound them, soul to soul.

Afterwards, he gently lowered himself beside her, and she held him close, their bodies still entwined in a quiet, comforting embrace. Eventually, he eased away, the space between them thick with the weight of their shared experience. Both breathed heavily, their chests rising and falling in perfect synchrony, the silence between them filled with the moment's intimacy.

They gazed into each other's eyes, a quiet understanding passing between them—a comfort they hadn't known they'd been searching for. That night, they found peace in each other's arms, marking a turning point for both.

The following day, Yolaine woke slowly, her body still humming with the memory of Pierce beside her. His bare form lay tangled in the sheets, the softness of his skin against hers lingering like an imprint. The night they shared had been more than physical—a collision of emotions, desires, and unspoken confessions. She felt a strange sense of peace and an undeniable pull to confront the unresolved things between them.

Her heart ached as she studied him, his features relaxed in sleep, the weight of their past hanging between them like a shadow. The past had been filled with mistakes, misunderstandings, and an affair that should never have happened—his, hers, theirs. The betrayal they had both suffered lingered between them, a silent presence they couldn't ignore. But at this moment, all of that seemed forgotten. The years of hurt, lies, and pain faded as the heat of their connection flared once more.

She slipped from his side quietly, careful not to disturb him, the need to breathe for a moment alone overwhelming her. Kaley would need to get ready for school, but her thoughts kept drifting back to Pierce, to the kiss they'd shared, the passion that had once been the bedrock of their relationship, now entwined with pain and confusion.

She entered the shower, hoping the water would wash away the heaviness that clung to her thoughts. But the second the spray hit her skin, she realised it wasn't the water that would change things—it was Pierce stepping in behind her.

He was warm, his body pressing against her back, his hands sliding over her damp skin as he pulled her close. His breath was hot against her ear, his lips trailing over her neck, a slow, deliberate kiss that sent a shiver down her spine. There were no words—no need for them. She could feel the hunger in his touch; the raw need mirrored her own. She had missed him, missed them, in an almost painful way.

His hands slid to her waist, fingers brushing against the curve of her hips, the touch possessive, like he was claiming what had always been his. Her breath hitched as he turned her to face him, his lips finding hers in a desperate kiss, bruising in its intensity. There was no gentleness in it—just pure, unfiltered need. His body pressed harder against hers, his hands sliding up to cup her face as if he were afraid she might slip away.

She kissed him back with equal urgency, her hands roaming over his body, reacquainting herself with the familiar yet thrilling sensation of being with him. The heat between them was overwhelming, the weight of their shared history both a burden and a promise. At this moment, there was no past, no betrayal—only the desperate, aching need to reconnect.

He broke the kiss, his lips trailing down her neck, over her collarbone, his hands exploring her body like it was the first time. Every touch and caress felt like a plea, a silent apology for everything they had lost. She responded in kind, her body arching into his touch, a fire igniting between them that nothing could quench.

As they stood there, their bodies entwined in the steam-filled shower, time seemed to stretch, the world outside forgotten. Slowly, they pulled away, their breaths ragged, their eyes meeting with something unspoken—an understanding. This moment had shifted something inside both of them. The connection they shared was fragile but undeniable.

After silence, Pierce reached for the towel, his fingers lingering on her skin. She did the same, drying him off slowly, deliberately, as if they were trying to savour every second of the closeness, every inch of the intimacy they had rediscovered.

When the moment ended and they were both dressed, Pierce kissed her softly, a brief but lingering touch that spoke volumes. He was leaving for his flight, but his gaze was now soft—a tenderness that hadn't been there before. Yolaine felt it too, the tentative hope that maybe, just maybe, they could find their way back to each other.

He turned to her as he walked toward the door, offering a quiet wave. The tension between them had eased, but there was still much to face. The path ahead was uncertain, but at that moment, there was a fragile promise that things might still work out.

Yolaine turned to wake Kaley, her heart lighter but still full of the weight of the journey ahead.

## #16
# The Lies We Live

Pierce had been away on a business trip for several days, and as often happened in his absence, Yolaine immersed herself in work and the daily tasks of caring for Kaley. She drew comfort from the routine, its familiar rhythm a steady anchor. Kaley was the heart of her world, and Yolaine cherished every moment with her daughter, watching her grow and change. It gave her purpose, a structure to hold her steady. Yet alongside it crept quiet isolation, as if the outside world had slipped into the background.

Despite the distance, Yolaine hadn't entirely severed ties with Aston. She hadn't cut him off completely. They stayed in touch, swapping messages occasionally, and sometimes, their exchanges carried a subtle flirtation, an undeniable spark simmering beneath. Yolaine wasn't sure where it might lead, but Aston was more than just a lover to her. He was a friend—a confidant who listened and made her feel valued in ways she hadn't felt in ages. Even now, as she worked to mend things with Pierce, Yolaine couldn't quite let Aston go. There was a bond there she wasn't ready to break, a connection that brought her comfort and understanding. She liked him, and that wasn't something she'd abandon just because Pierce was back.

Yolaine wasn't one to socialise much, especially not with neighbours or other people. She preferred solitude, keeping life simple. She had no interest in gossip or the shallow conversations that came with gatherings. Her friends, if she could call them that, were few—mostly acquaintances from work or brief encounters. Janice was different, though. Janice had been her closest friend for years, someone Yolaine trusted without hesitation, who'd stood by her throughout her life. She knew Yolaine's secrets, pain, joys, and struggles. More importantly, Janice understood Yolaine's bitterness, why she kept her distance from others, and why she stayed closed off.

For all her warmth and openness, Janice was the one Yolaine leaned on in fragile moments. She knew about Yolaine's affairs over the years, though Yolaine always insisted they were just a way to get back at Pierce. The truth was, Yolaine had often felt neglected and unappreciated by her husband, whose own betrayals were nothing new. Pierce had never been the faithful husband—his infidelity an open secret she couldn't ignore, even if he mostly kept it hidden. There were slips, moments when Yolaine uncovered the truth, and that's when the cracks in their marriage widened. Instead of confronting him, she'd sought solace in others' arms, hoping to fill the emptiness inside. It was a cycle they'd both fuelled, hiding behind lies, retreating deeper into themselves.

The doorbell rang just as Yolaine got home from work, tending to Kaley and settling her for the evening. She wasn't expecting anyone. Glancing at the clock, she sighed—likely Janice. They hadn't seen each other in a while, and though Yolaine always welcomed her company, a strange tension hung in the air tonight, an unease she couldn't shake.

Opening the door, Yolaine saw Janice on the doorstep, looking slightly uneasy, as if she'd wavered about coming. Janice offered a soft smile, but hesitation in her eyes made Yolaine pause—something subtle but off.

"Yolaine, love," Janice began, her voice gentle yet tinged with an unfamiliar weight as she stepped inside, Yolaine easing out of the way. "I'm sorry to just turn up like this, but I must talk to you. There's something I've been keeping from you."

Yolaine's brow furrowed, concern flickering over her face. Janice had always been upfront, never shying from the truth, no matter how tough. So what was this now, this thing she'd held back? A knot of foreboding tightened in her stomach.

They drifted into the living room, where Kaley played happily on the floor, oblivious to the heaviness settling in. Yolaine sank onto the couch, her mind racing, and Janice joined her, posture tense. The room was quiet, but for Kaley's soft humming, it was a stark contrast to the looming conversation.

Yolaine turned to Janice, heart pounding. "What's going on, Janice?" she asked, her voice softer now, though uncertainty lingered.

Janice hesitated at the threshold, her eyes flickering nervously as if wrestling with whether to speak. Yolaine noticed the discomfort in her friend's stance and the subtle strain in her expression. Janice had always been open, never one to hide the truth, no matter how difficult. But now, something felt different—a pause like this could shift everything. When she spoke, her voice was gentle, almost apologetic, bracing for the fallout.

"It's about Pierce," Janice said, her voice carrying a tone that Yolaine couldn't quite decipher. "Martin saw him with another woman yesterday while at a retreat with his friends."

Yolaine's heart skipped a beat, the words striking her like an electric shock, but she kept herself composed, forcing the rising panic down. "What do you mean?" she asked, calm but edged with disbelief. She couldn't allow herself to believe it—not yet.

Janice looked briefly at the floor, her fingers twisting nervously at the hem of her shirt. "He and this woman... they were holding hands. Sitting just a little away from Martin and his friends, almost as though they were... a couple." The words hung in the air, heavy and suffocating, as Janice met her gaze again.

Yolaine's mind went blank, thoughts racing in all directions, but on the outside, she remained calm, shaking her head as though denying the truth. "It must've been someone else, Janice. You don't know for sure it was him. We've been working things out. He promised... he promised he wouldn't do this again. He wouldn't."

Janice's face softened with concern, her eyes searching Yolaine's as if trying to convey her empathy. "I know you want to believe that, Yolaine. But Martin saw them—he saw them together. I couldn't keep this from you. I just couldn't."

Yolaine's pulse hammered in her ears, the weight of the revelation sinking in. She'd just started to believe that Pierce had changed, that they were rebuilding something solid and tangible for her and Kaley. Just days ago, they had shared a quiet, hopeful moment, a fresh start, a last chance. But now, this news shattered that fragile hope. The sting of betrayal was sharp, even before it fully sank in.

Janice pressed on, her voice trembling, each word fragile. "I wasn't supposed to tell you. Martin asked me not to get involved or say anything, but I couldn't stay quiet. You deserve to know."

Yolaine sat in stillness, her face unreadable. She didn't shout, cry, or flinch. Her emotions churned beneath the surface, locked behind a calm façade. The room felt more minor, the quiet hum of Kaley fading into the background as her mind raced.

Janice watched her nervously, waiting for a response, any sign of emotion. But Yolaine remained composed, her calmness masking the storm inside. The silence stretched between them, thick and uncomfortable.

Finally, Yolaine spoke, her voice low and controlled. "Which retreat?"

"Swiss Inn," Janice replied.

Yolaine nodded slowly, her gaze sharp. "Don't tell anyone about this," she said, her eyes locking onto Janice's with a chilling intensity. "I'll deal with it when Pierce gets back."

Janice nodded, her shoulders sagging in relief, though a lingering worry remained in her eyes. "I just wanted you to know, Yolaine. I'm so sorry."

Yolaine rose, her body stiff, her mind still in turmoil. "I'll handle it," she whispered, almost to herself. "Thank you for telling me."

As Janice left, Yolaine stood frozen, the space around her suddenly vast, her world quietly tilting. She didn't know what to believe anymore. The man she had trusted, the one she thought she was rebuilding her life with, was slipping away from her grasp. The foundation she had believed was solid now felt like quicksand. She wasn't sure who Pierce was—or who she was becoming in this tangled web of lies. But one thing was sure: the fragile calm she'd fought to maintain was on the brink of shattering, and she would have to face whatever came next.

She sat down on the couch, her thoughts a whirlwind. After a long pause, she picked up her phone and dialled Pierce. No answer. She tried again, and this time, he picked up.

"Hello," Pierce answered, his voice lazy and casual, as though nothing was wrong.

Yolaine took a deep breath, her voice quiet and calm as she asked, "What are you doing?"

"I'm on my bed," Pierce replied, almost too relaxed. Then, trying to shift the focus of the conversation, he added, "How's Kaley? Is she asleep?"

Yolaine didn't respond to his question; instead, she pressed forward with the one weighing her mind. "Are you alone?" she asked, her tone sharp, the suspicion bubbling beneath the surface.

"Very much so," Pierce answered, but Yolaine knew immediately that he was lying. The way his voice shifted, just slightly, gave it away. Her anger flared. She had been giving him the benefit of the doubt for far too long, but this time was different.

Her voice turned cold, each word cutting through the tension in the air. "Hope the woman next to you knows you're married and have your commitments," she said, her eyes narrowing as she waited for his reaction.

There was a moment of silence on the other end of the line, and then Pierce spoke, his voice a little shakier now. "What are you talking about, Yolaine?"

Yolaine's voice remained steady, though there was a hard edge to it now. "Swiss Inn is a nice place to spend your time," she said pointedly, each syllable deliberate, aimed at the heart of the betrayal she had uncovered.

Pierce's response was immediate silence. He knew. He knew she had figured it out. He knew she was no longer in the dark, willing to ignore what was happening right before her. The realisation hit him hard, yet there was nothing he could say to fix it. The silence stretched between them, thick and suffocating, the kind that only comes when the truth is so evident that even words feel unnecessary.

Yolaine didn't need him to speak. The silence spoke for him, louder than any defence or excuse he could offer. She didn't cry. She didn't weep. She remained strong, the weight of the moment settling over her with a clarity she hadn't had before. She ended the call without another word, her finger pressing the red button decisively, cutting the connection as she stared at the phone screen in her hand as though it might offer some answer. But there was nothing.

For a long while, Yolaine sat there, her mind racing through all the things she had ignored, the doubts she had pushed aside. Slowly, she gathered herself. There was nothing more to be said. She knew what she had to do.

Later that night, she climbed into Kaley's room, finding solace in the warmth of her daughter's presence. She curled up beside her, holding her close, the only anchor in a world that was suddenly starting to crumble. Kaley was the one constant, the one thing Yolaine could still trust.

The following day, Yolaine packed her things. The decision had been made. She would not stay in that house, not any longer. She wouldn't continue to try to make a life with someone who had betrayed her so completely.

Yolaine left, her bags packed, her resolve firm. She didn't look back as she walked away from Pierce, from the life they had built together. It was over. She was determined to start anew, to make a life for herself and Kaley, free from the lies and deceit that had come to define her marriage. She had given him countless chances, but she had compromised herself for too long by trying to provoke him, hoping he would change. Not anymore.

This time, Yolaine was different. She was done being hurt. I'm done waiting for things to get better. False promises or empty apologies wouldn't sway her. Pierce knew it, too. He didn't try to stop her. And this time, Yolaine knew with certainty there was no turning back.

# Gossip – Some say it was true

Books One and Two of Unfaithful Desires are grounded in a rich blend of gossip, real-life events, and a creative exploration of human emotions. While certain parts of the story were drawn from the imagination, much of it reflected the authentic experiences of the characters—their ways of living, loving, and interacting with one another. Through these interactions, we saw how the words whispered behind closed doors, the shared secrets and the lies were spun into narratives that shaped the destinies of each person. Gossip, fueling so many stories, was central in propelling this tale forward. It weaved through family ties, friendships, and the tangled web of relationships, turning simple exchanges into life-altering moments.

The narrative of *Unfaithful Desires* picks apart the pieces of its characters' lives, showing how their paths often cross unexpectedly. As they lived, they encountered one another in moments of joy, pain, and betrayal. Yet, it wasn't just their actions that mattered—how others perceived them and how their lives were interpreted through the lens of rumour and innuendo. Secrets were invented, exaggerated, and shared, each leaving its mark on the lives of those involved.

Aston, for example, had once been a significant part of Yolaine's life. He had been someone who had shared her dreams and passions, a man who had walked alongside her through some of her most pivotal moments. But, somewhere along the way, he lost his way. Aston felt a bottomless emptiness, a loss of direction that pulled him away from everything he had known. Once a cornerstone of his life, the church no longer held the answers he sought. To rebuild, he left his old life behind and embraced a new path of spirituality and service to others. He joined a Christian community, dedicating himself to a life of prayer and service, hoping to find meaning in a life of self-sacrifice. But with his new direction came the decision to leave Yolaine behind. He never reached out to her again, unable to reconcile the past with his new life. Yolaine, once central to his world, now felt like a distant memory that no longer fit into the framework of his spiritual rebirth.

Then, there was Glen, Yolaine's cousin, who had taken a different approach to life. After finishing his higher education, Glen moved abroad, seeking better opportunities. His hard work paid off, and he eventually secured a stable job. Over time, he built a life for himself, even falling in love and marrying a woman he adored. He became a father, settling into the rhythm of family life. Despite his new commitments and the distance between them, Glen maintained a connection with Yolaine, though the frequency of their interactions waned. They were family, and their bond remained—unbroken, yet distant, as time and life moved them further apart.

Eugene, too, had chosen a path that led him far from home. He married and settled abroad, building a life with his own family. His days were filled with the responsibilities that came with his new life, but he and Yolaine kept in touch occasionally. Though their friendship was no longer as frequent as it once had been, it endured. Eugene's life was stable and peaceful, and while he and Yolaine shared a history, that past was long behind them. Both had moved on, each with their families and new chapters to embrace. Despite their complicated past, Eugene maintained contact with his older brother, Pierce. He knew all too well how Pierce had taken Yolaine from him—not once but twice—always showing that he was better suited for her in every way: career, wealth, and the effortless charm that had drawn her in. But Eugene had long since let go of any bitterness. He lived his life, forgave Pierce for the past, and focused on his happiness and contentment in the life he had built.

Janice's story, however, took a more painful turn. She had once been in a relationship with Martin, and things seemed to be going well. But Martin's actions—his lies and betrayals—ultimately drove a wedge between them. When Janice discovered his infidelity, she chose to leave him. The pain of that decision wasn't manageable, but Janice knew she couldn't stay with someone who had disrespected her trust. She packed her belongings and moved away, taking her daughter, Caro. Despite the support Yolaine had shown her during the tough days of her separation, Janice and Yolaine gradually lost touch. Janice rebuilt her life, focusing on her career and raising Caro as a single mother. She never remarried; instead, she lived independently and found peace in her company.

But of all the relationships, perhaps the most complicated was the one between Yolaine and Pierce. Desires drove Pierce—his need for control was just as potent as his desire for power. For him, life was about winning, about having what he wanted, no matter the cost. Yolaine was the prize, the trophy he felt entitled to. He was possessive of her, and his manipulations were subtle but effective. He managed to pull her away from Eugene, not once, but twice. Their relationship, full of turbulence and passion, consumed them both. A constant battle marked Pierce's love for Yolaine for control, and it wasn't long before their dynamic became toxic.

Pierce was so consumed by his desire to possess Yolaine that he abandoned his life in Denmark—his job, his affairs, and his ambitions—to ensure that Yolaine wouldn't slip away again. When he learned that Yolaine and Eugene had reconciled, Pierce's obsession with her returned. He couldn't let her go. He couldn't bear the thought of losing his grip on her. And so, despite their separation, Pierce played a part in Yolaine's life, mainly regarding their daughter. Though divorced, he maintained a relationship with his child, and Yolaine didn't stop him from being a father. However, despite his role as a father, Pierce could not reconcile his feelings for Yolaine. The marriage had ended, and though he had no intention of remarrying, he continued to indulge in affairs, living life on his terms. His greatest regret, however, was being unable to control Yolaine completely. She slipped from his grasp, the ultimate failure for someone as controlling as Pierce. He willed his property to his daughter, Kaley, naming her as the beneficiary. His love for her remained unwavering, a constant in his life, despite everything else that had changed.

As for Yolaine, she had finally found the strength to move on. The pain of her past with Pierce had left scars, but she refused to let them define her. She focused on her work, partnering with her brother, Edward, in his fashion design firm. Together, they built something meaningful, something that gave her life purpose. And then there was Kaley, Yolaine's daughter, who became her rock. Kaley was Yolaine's world, her constant companion and source of joy. Yolaine chose to live a life free from the chaos of short flings or meaningless relationships. She didn't need that anymore. She had found peace in her work and her daughter.

Eventually, Yolaine remarried. After filing for divorce, Pierce reluctantly agreed to let her go. She found a kind and decent partner who offered stability and support. She had two more children with him, and for the first time in years, Yolaine experienced the joy of a peaceful family life. But despite the peace, rumours still swirled around her. There were whispers of her having affairs even after her remarriage, but the truth of these allegations was never clear. Gossip spread like wildfire, but Yolaine had long learned to ignore it. People loved to talk and create stories based on what they saw or heard. Whether the rumours were true or not, Yolaine didn't let them affect her. She had moved on.

From my perspective as an observer, I can't help but reflect on the dynamic between Yolaine and Pierce. They were two people who thrived on excitement, on living life by their own rules. They loved the luxury of their desires and the challenge of controlling their world. Their relationship wasn't just about love but power, control, and the thrill of getting what they wanted. They were drawn to each other for reasons beyond mere affection, and their lives together became a series of calculated risks and rewards.

Ultimately, their actions—intentional or not—had far-reaching consequences. Their desires, need for control, and passion for each other affected everyone around them. Rumours of a couple swap, dangerous liaisons, and risky behaviour only added to the drama of their story. But it wasn't just about the truth but how people interpreted what they saw and heard. Gossip, whether grounded in fact or fantasy, shaped perceptions and Yolaine and Pierce's lives were an open canvas for speculation.

No matter how much I tried to distance myself from the rumours and gossip, the truth remained that people would always form their judgments based on what they'd heard. And, as with most stories, the truth became a mystery—lost in the whispers of those who didn't know the whole story. Those around them were inevitably affected, each paying a price in one way or another. Whether through emotional distress, shattered relationships, or the far-reaching consequences of their decisions, no one was untouched by the aftermath of Yolaine and Pierce's choices. Their lives were defined by passion, mistakes, love, loss, and the consequences of their actions. The legacy they left behind was one of unforgettable desires, forever marked in the lives of those who had crossed their paths.

www.ingramcontent.com/pod-product-compliance
Lightning Source LLC
LaVergne TN
LVHW041706070526
838199LV00045B/1228